O THE WONDER
of it all

A Seasonal Photo Journey of the Ozarks

Rosalie Perryman

Copyright © 2023 Rosalee Perryman
All cover art copyright © 2023 Rosalee Perryman
All Rights Reserved

No part of this book may be reproduced or transmitted in any form or by any means, electronic or mechanical, including photocopying, recording, or by any information storage and retrieval system, without permission in writing from the author/photographer.

Publishing Coordinator – Sharon Kizziah-Holmes

Paperback-Press
an imprint of A & S Publishing
Paperback Press, LLC

ISBN -13: 978-1-960499-15-8

ACKNOWLEDGEMENTS

Want to thank my husband Dalton of 60+ years for being the driver for most of the photo shoots taken in the Ozarks. He has always been ready to go whenever I said, "How about a photo shoot today?" Never complain about stopping when I say " I see a butterfly, stop… flowers stop … birds" or whatever I spot along our travels.

Also, I want to thank my daughters Debbie and Lois Ann for their encouragement and help to put this photo book together.

CONTENTS

SPRING 1-10

SUMMER 11-22

FALL 23-32

WINTER..................... 33-44

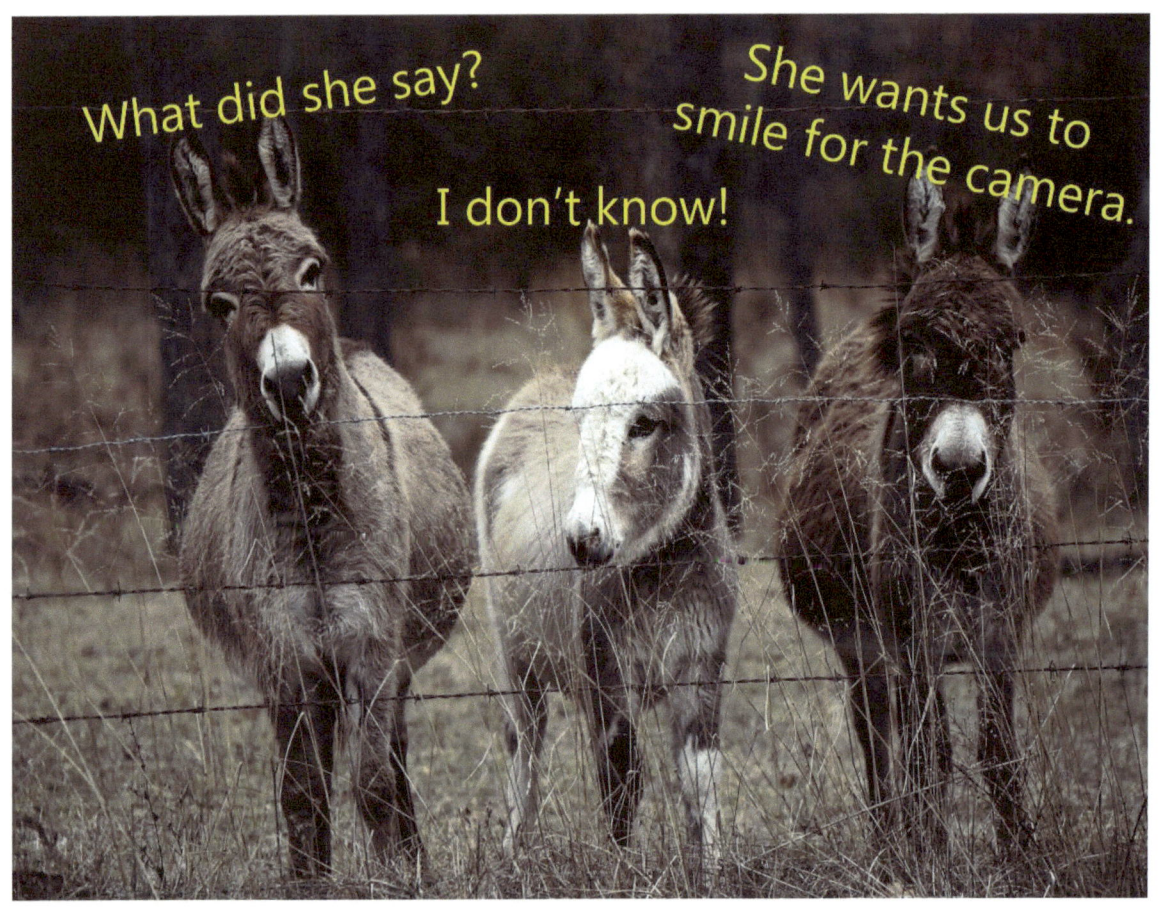

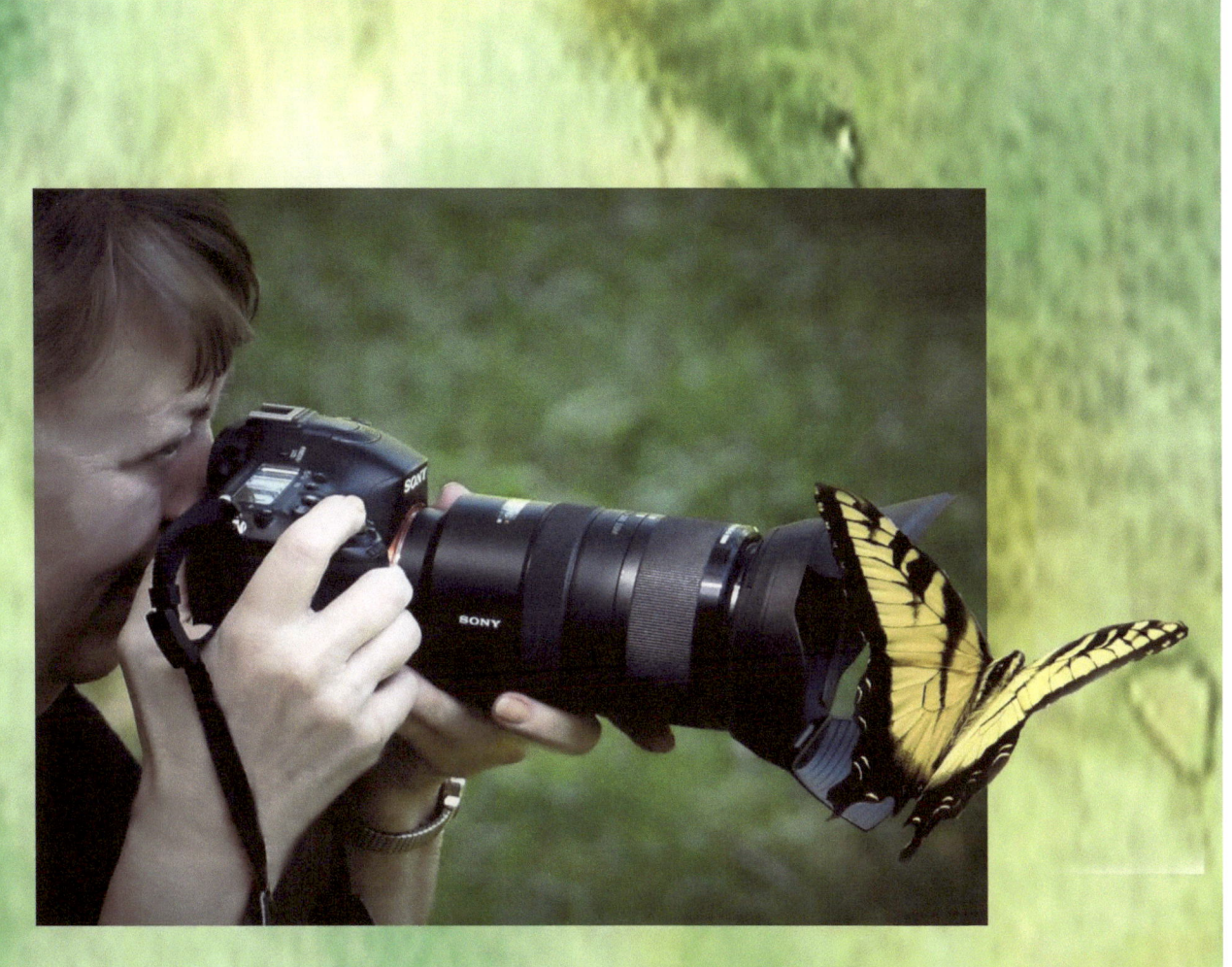

Spring is a time of new beginnings
and life cycle starting again.

We all need to take care of the gifts of nature
that God has created for us.
We can learn of God's love for us
through His creation.

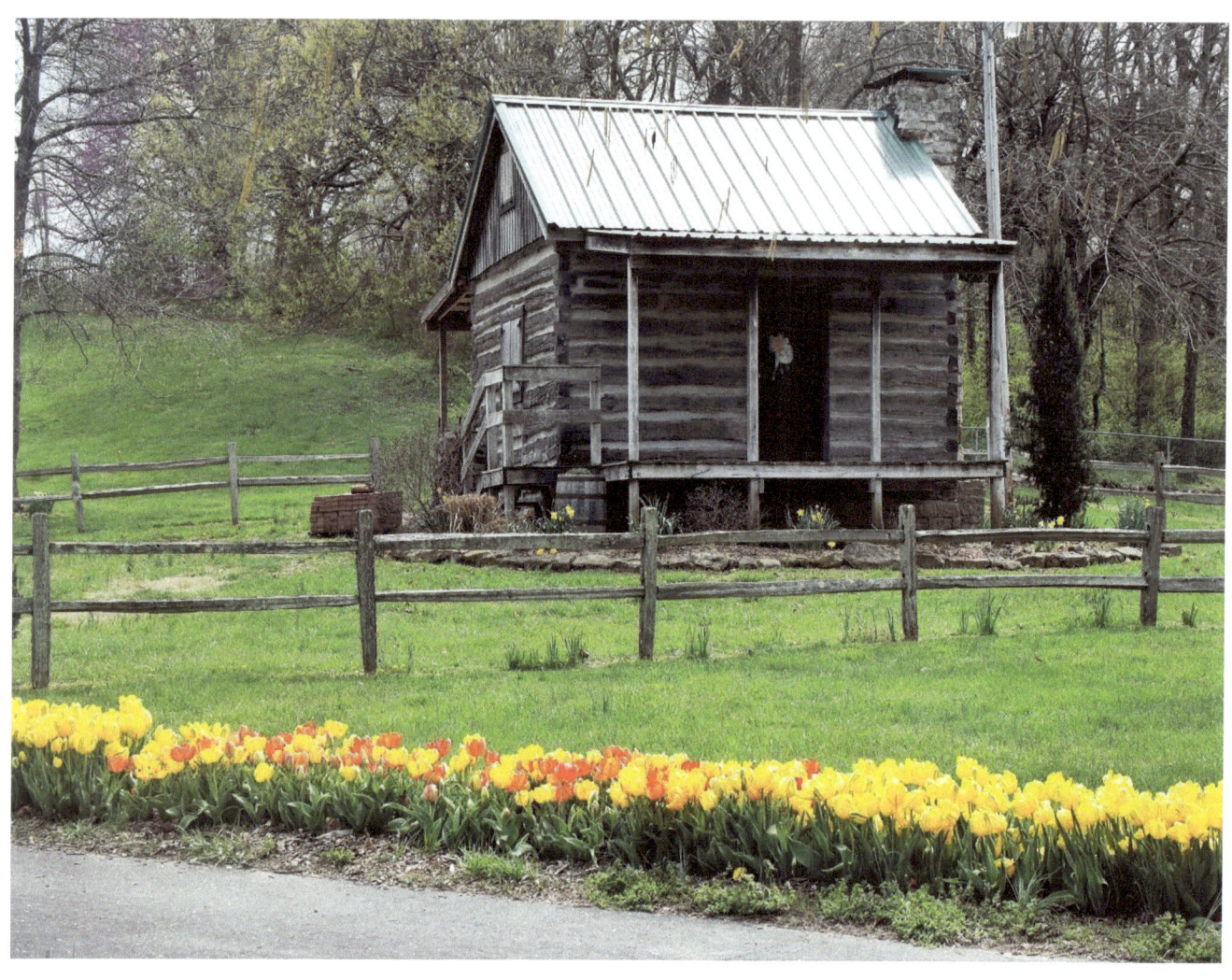

Spring Time

One lazy Spring afternoon, on a long trip making many
wonderful memories taking photos of Spring flowers,
we were blessed to see
colorful Tulips were in bloom again,
Daisies lined each side the roads, and
perfume scent from the Lilac trees was in the air.

Thank you God for a lovely Spring day.

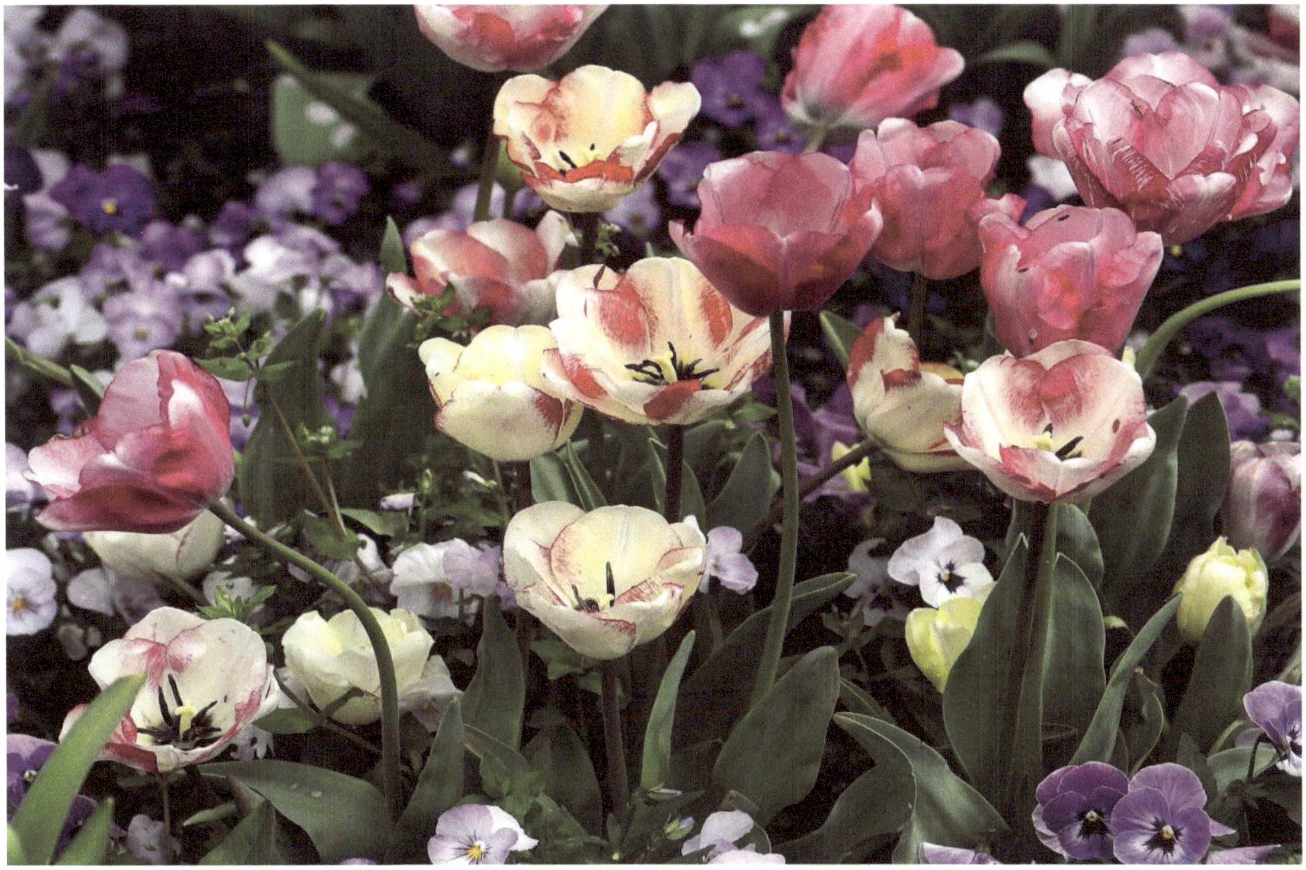

Spring arrives with great beauty.

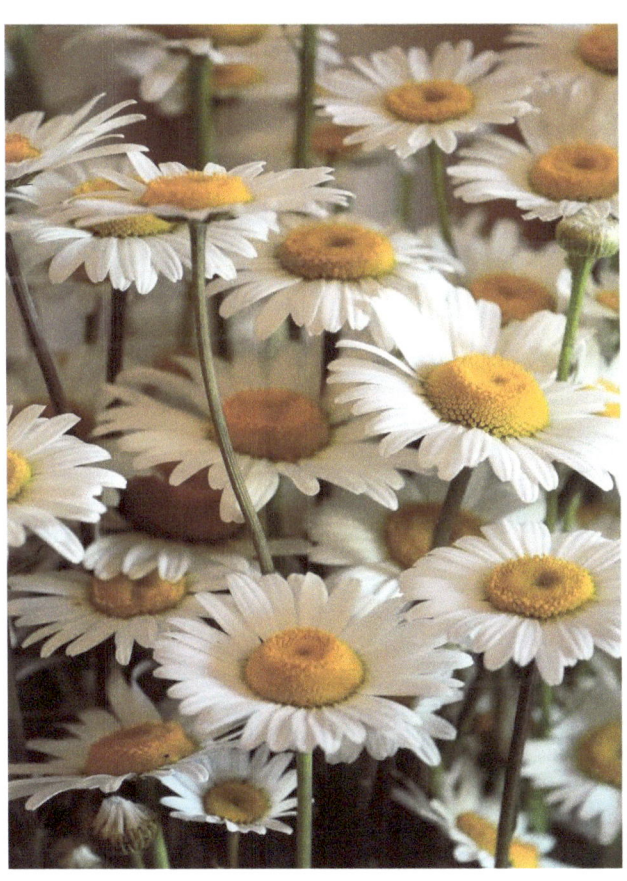

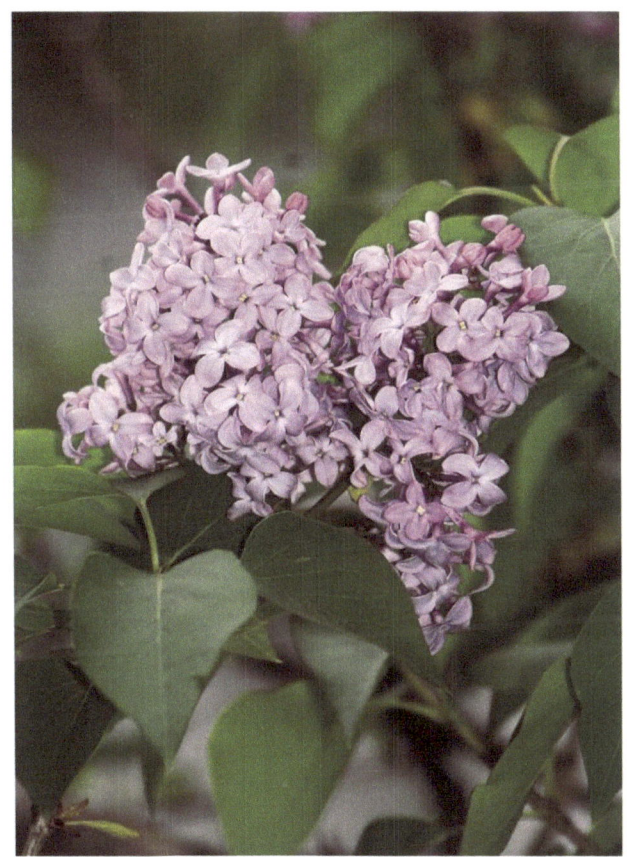

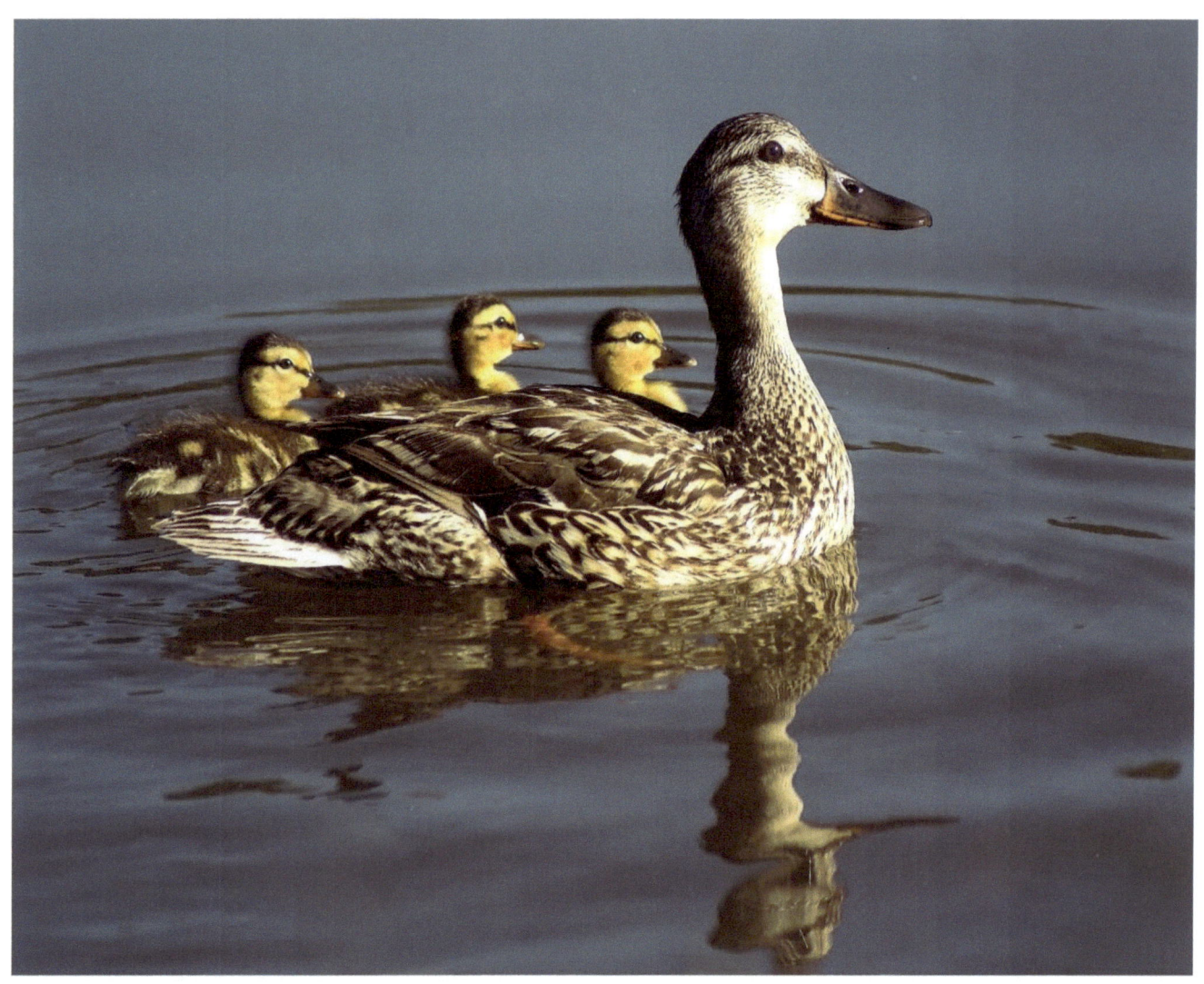

One lazy afternoon while out for a ride in country,

"Stop" "I see ducks on the pond."

The mother Mallard Duck didn't seem to mind me taking their picture, and she seemed very proud of her little ducklings.

God has created different kinds of birds and designed everything to work out according to His plan.

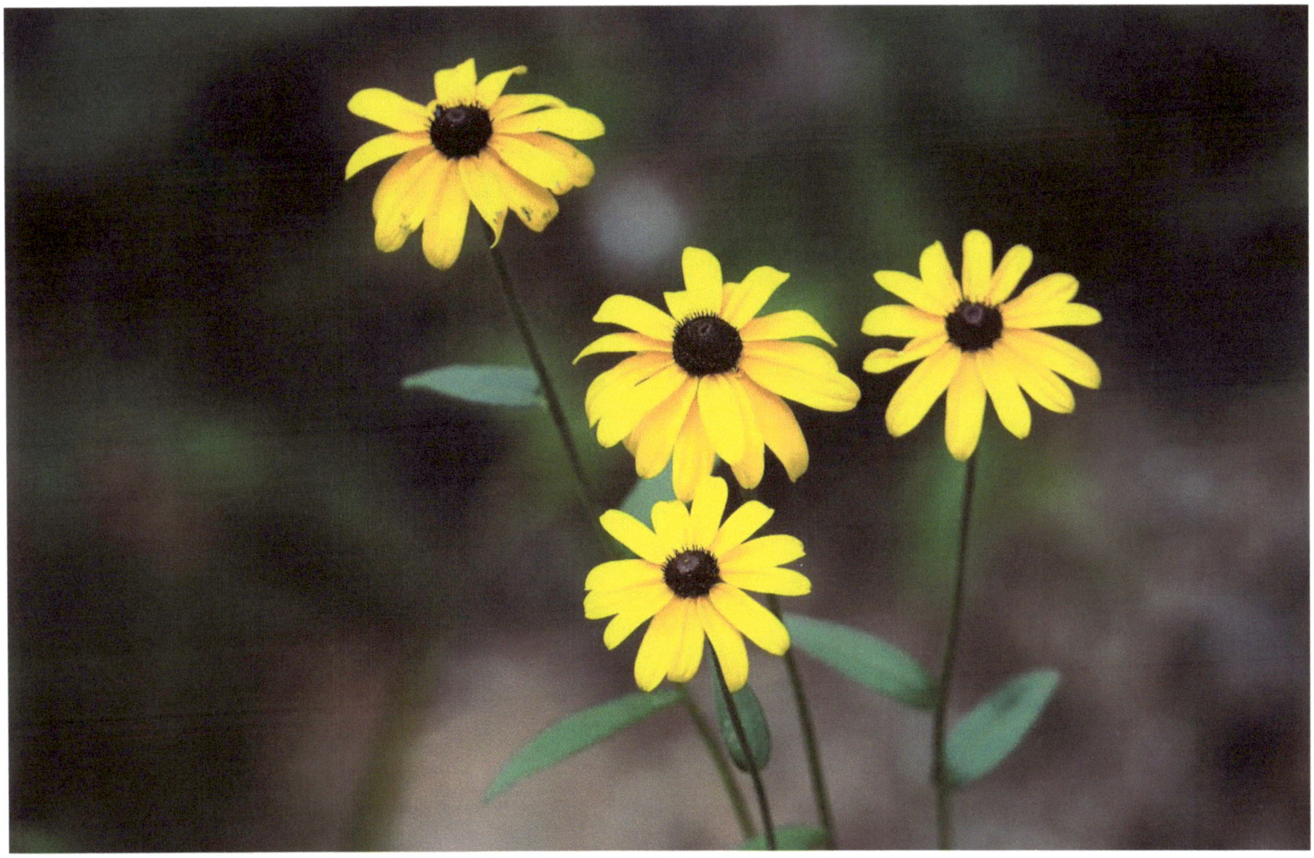

Spring Time

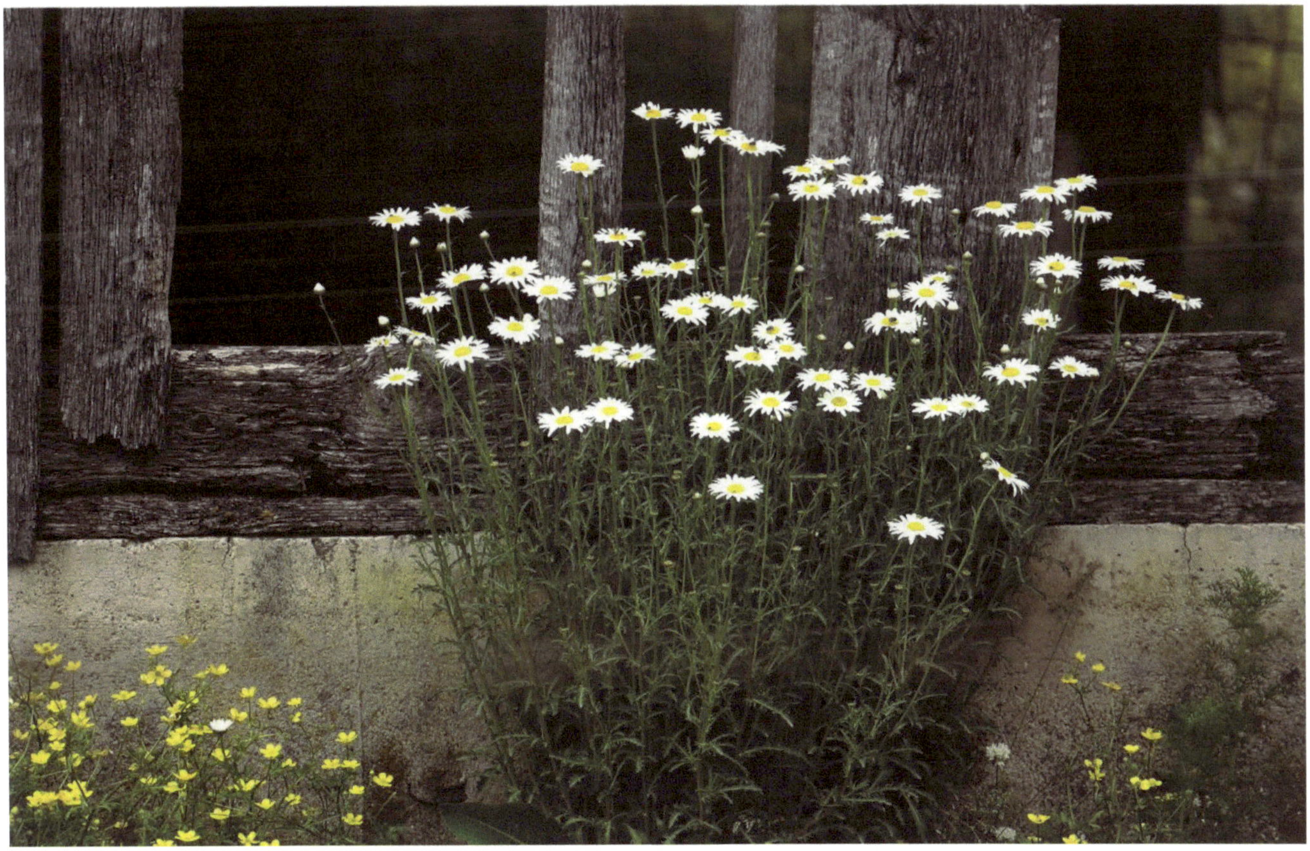

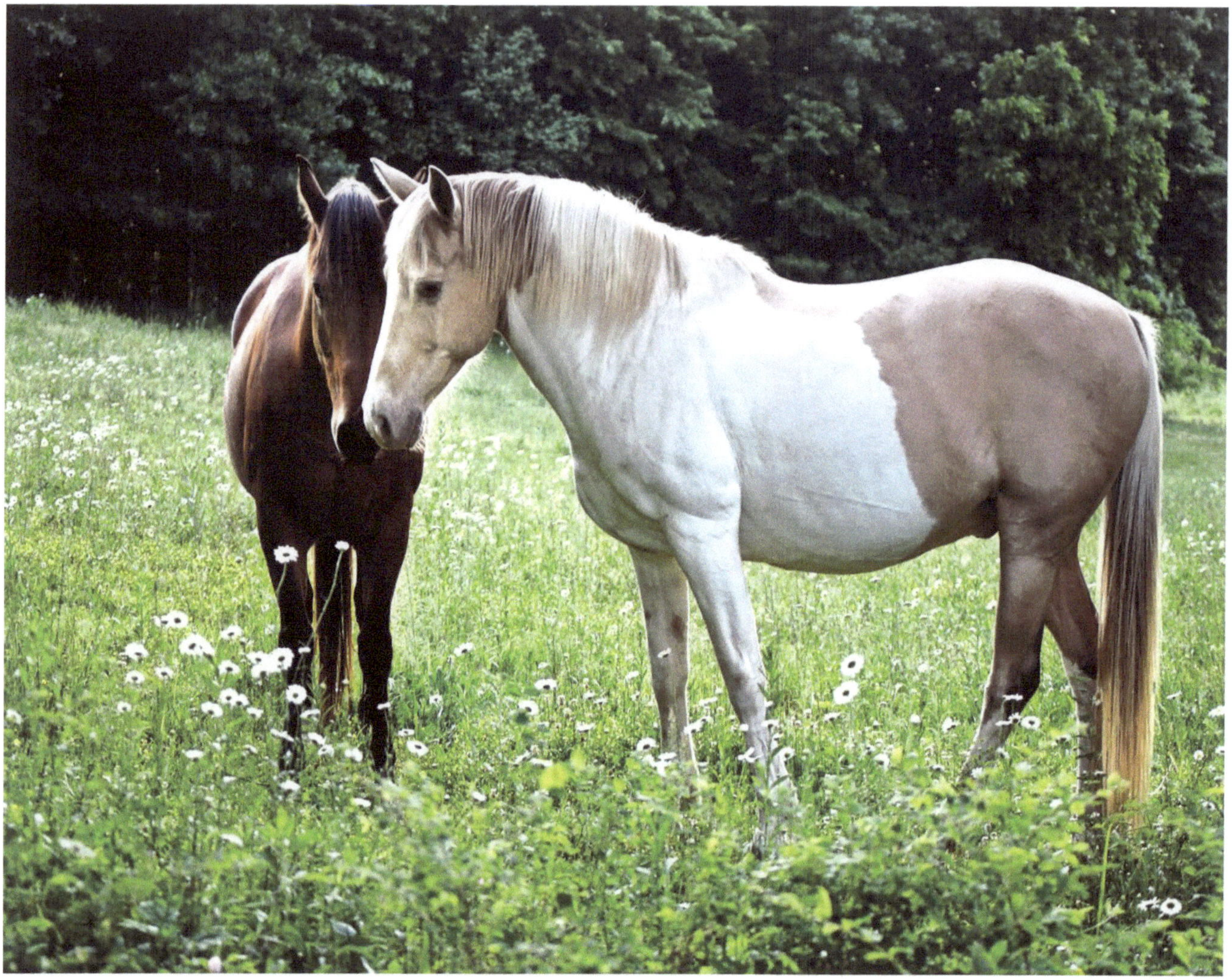

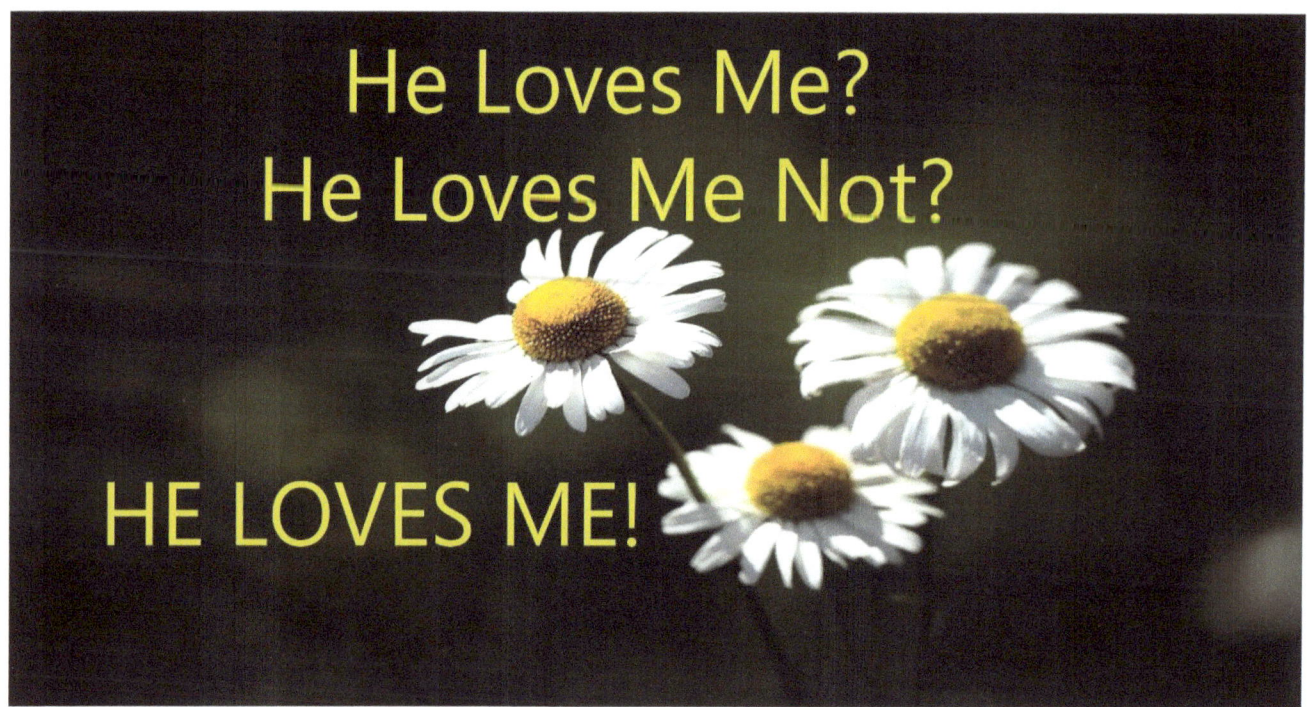

He Loves Me?
He Loves Me Not?

HE LOVES ME!

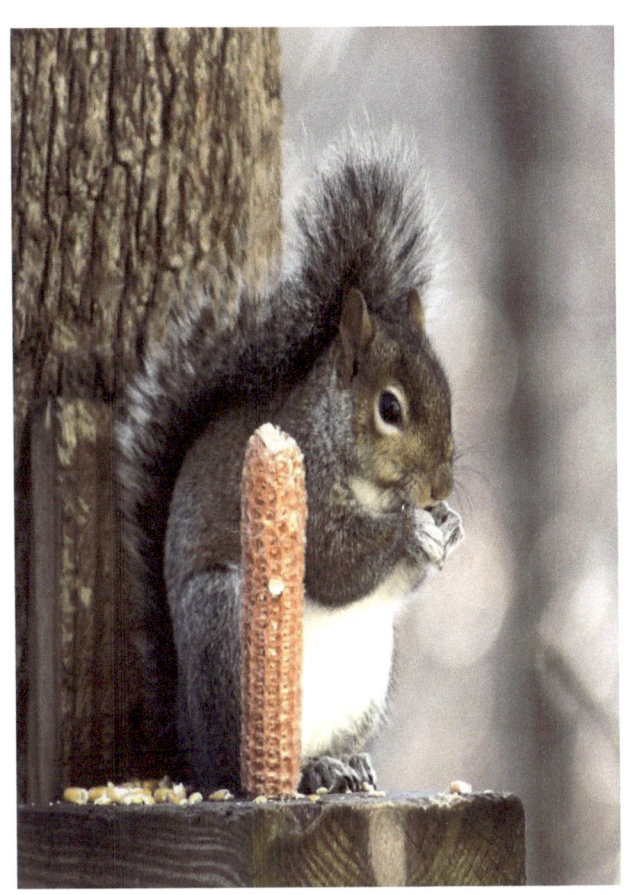 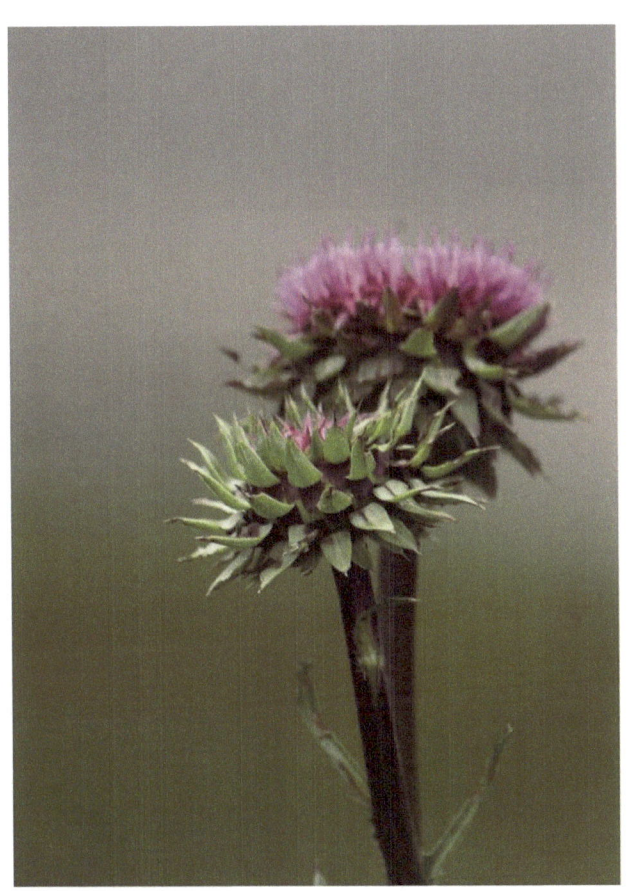

Nature is a thing of beauty and
God is the master artist of all his creations.

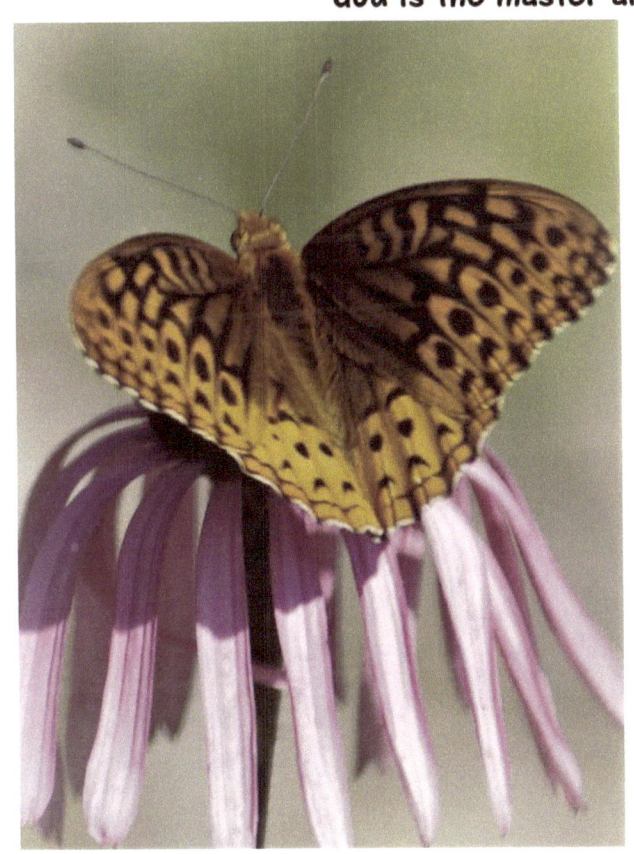 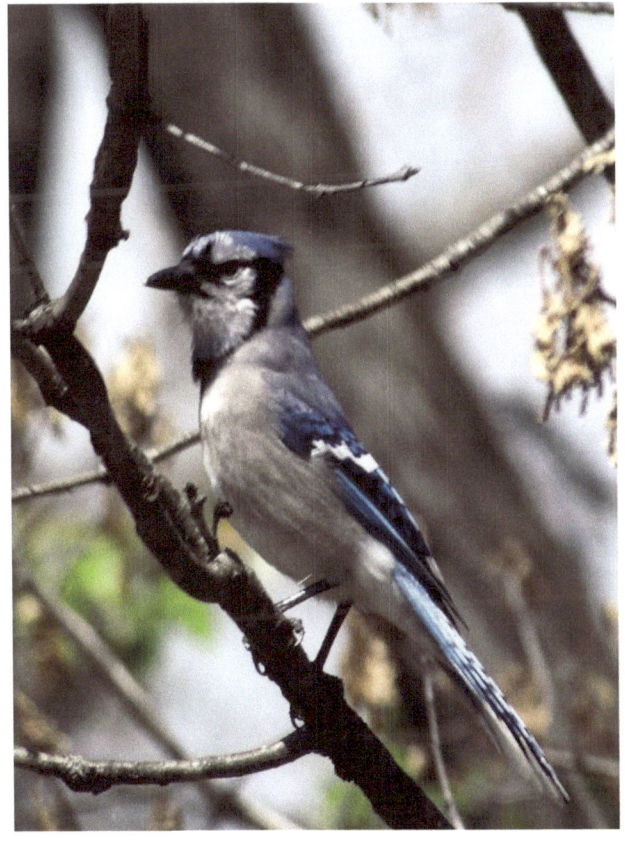

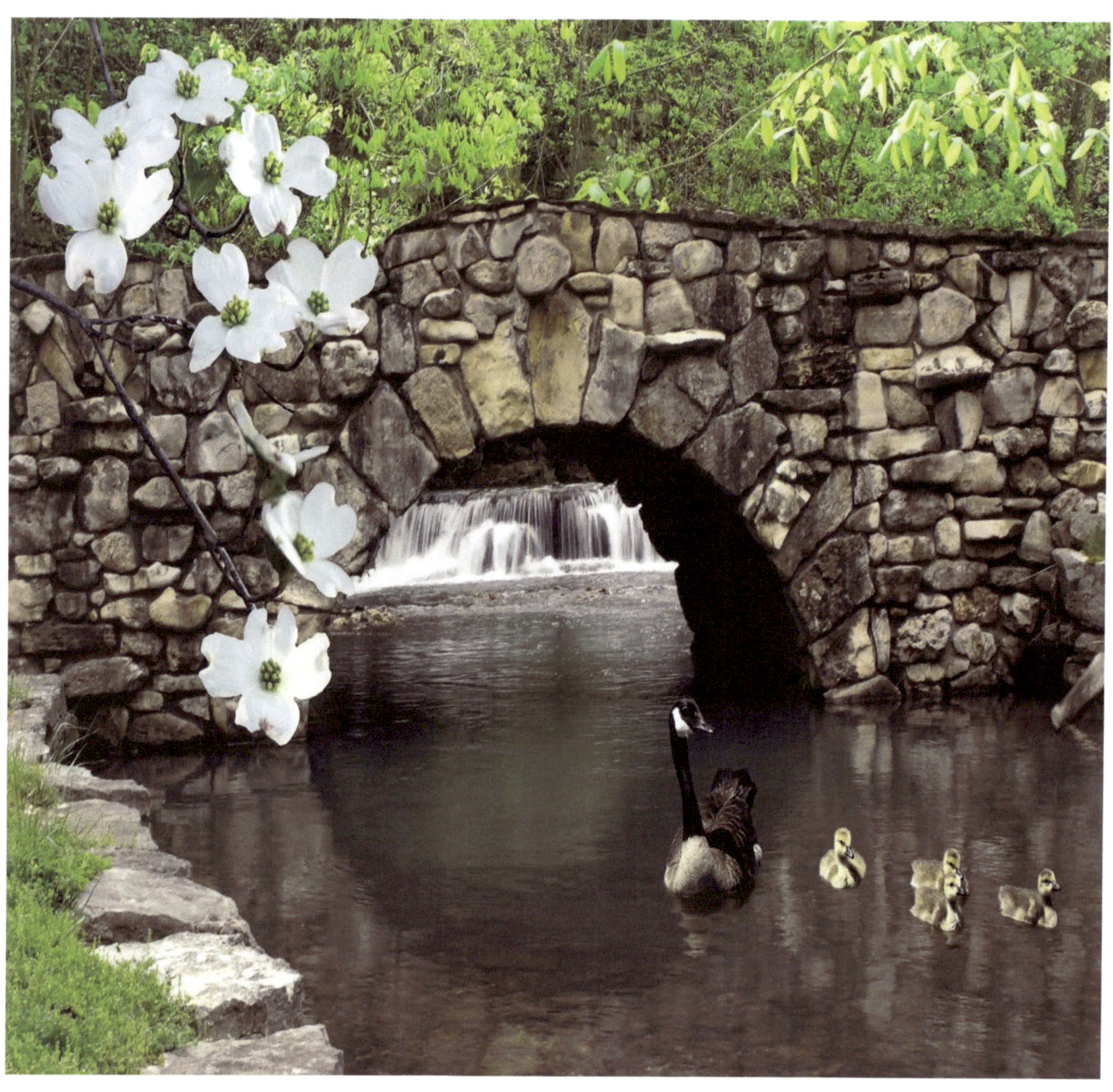

So I can remember and share God's artwork, I take photos as we journey through the country gravel roads.

On this day, we were blessed to see
a mother and her babies enjoying a peaceful Spring day.
Along the way also saw birds, butterflies, flowers, and much more.

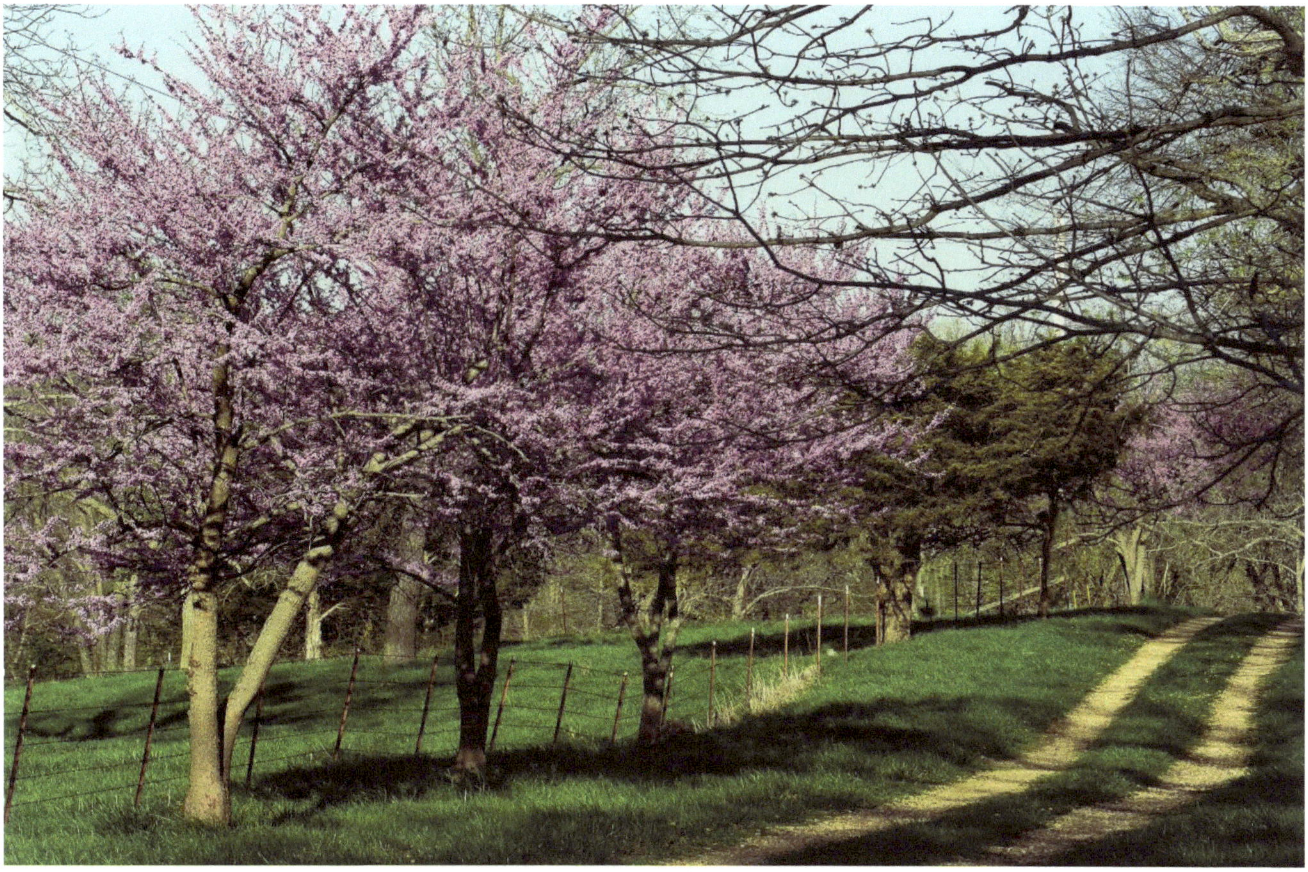

God paints for us all a wonderful world.

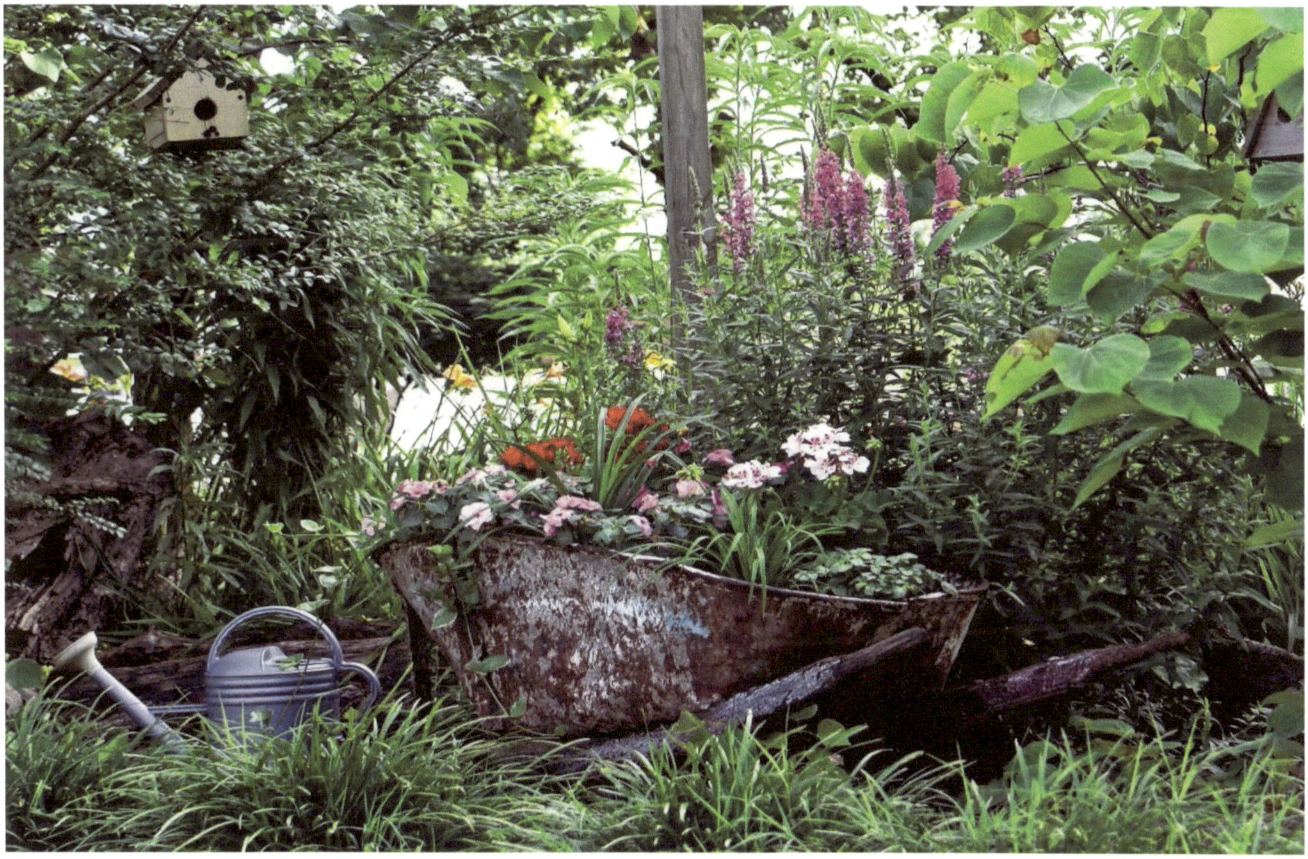

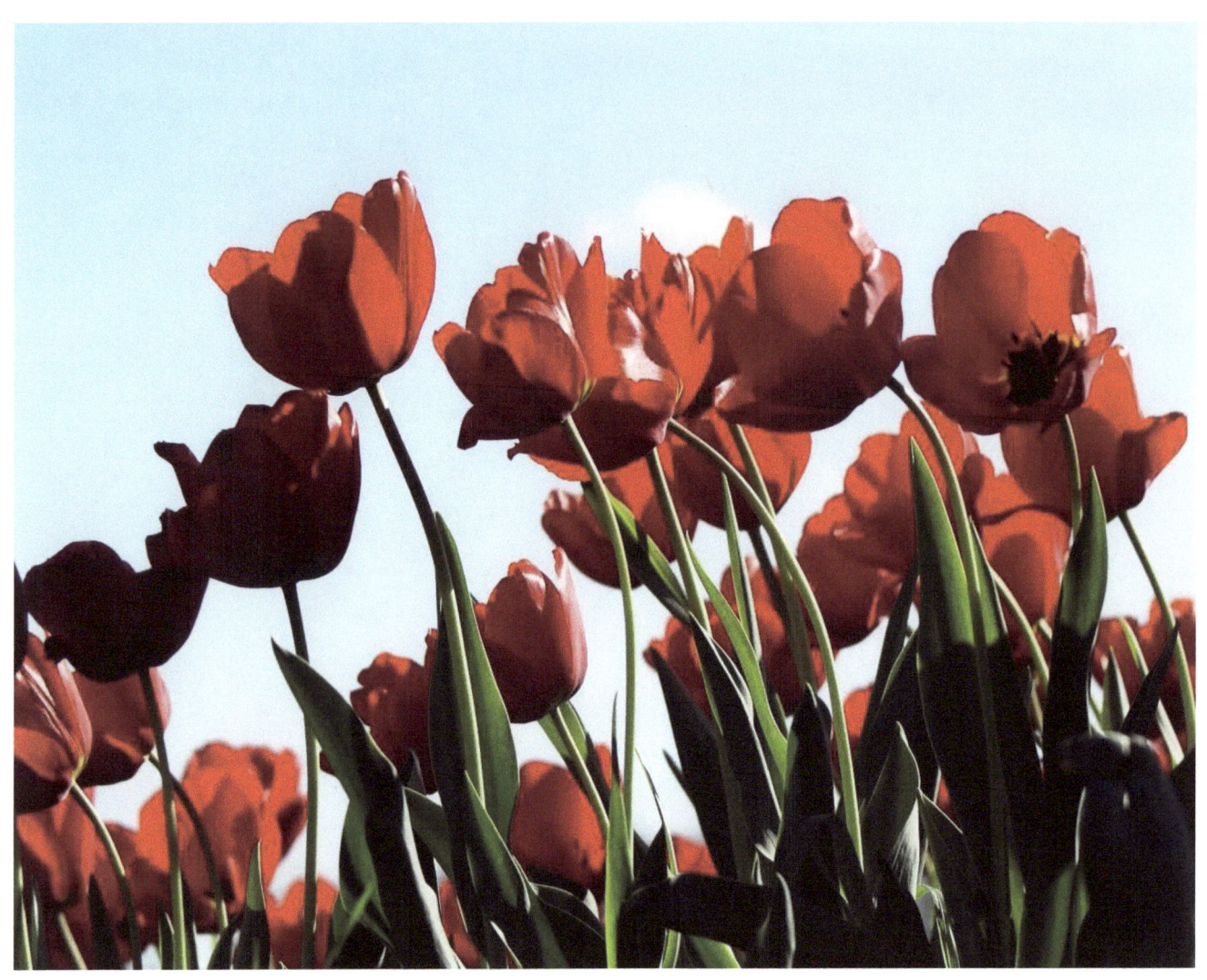

Over the rivers and down the road, driving we will go!

It's a bright sunshiny day and a soft gentle breeze in the air.

As I was looking around at the amazing world God had created,
I spotted these beautiful red Tulips in a farmer's yard.

Love all the bright colors that God uses
to paint flowers in the Springtime.

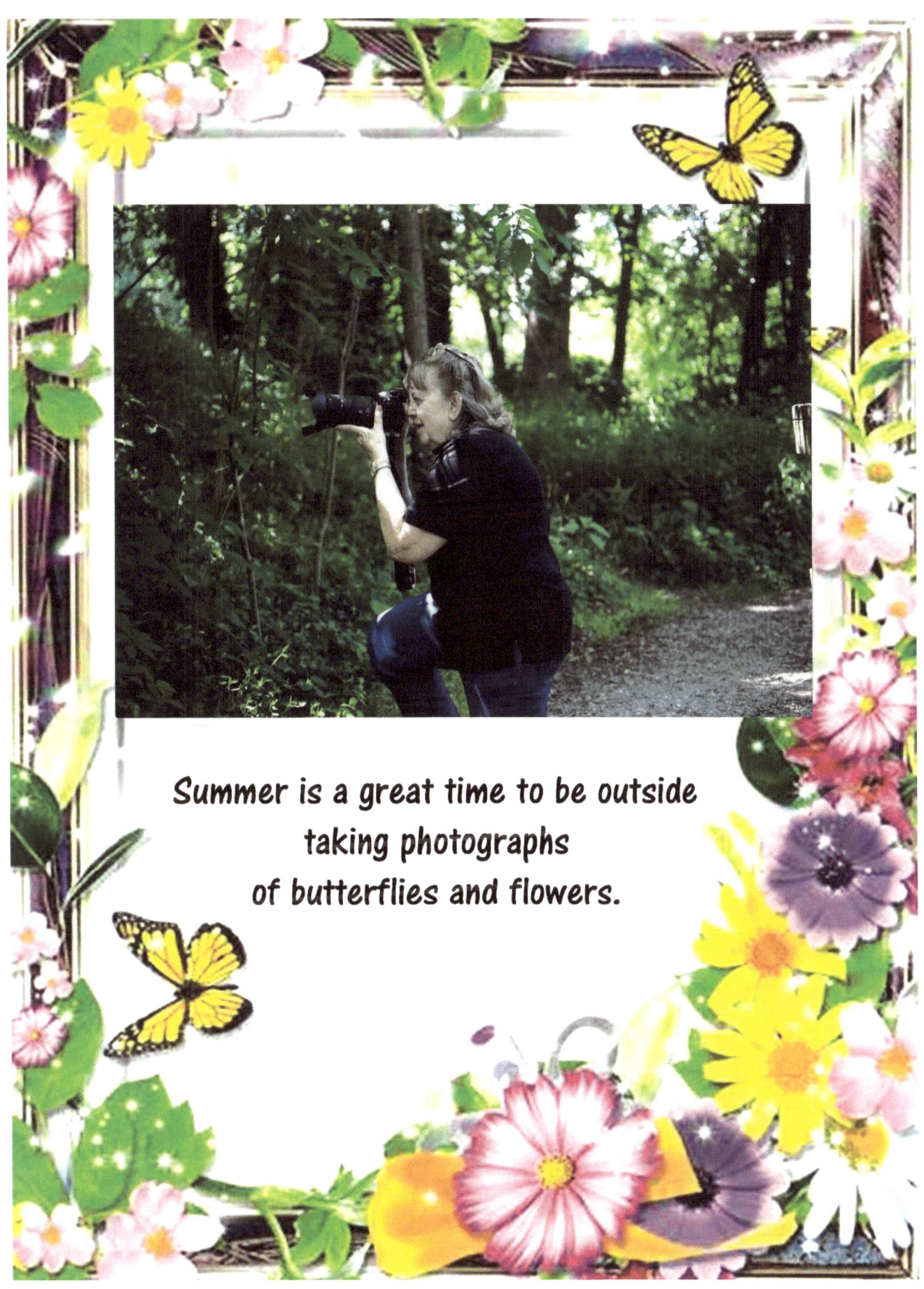

Summer is a great time to be outside
taking photographs
of butterflies and flowers.

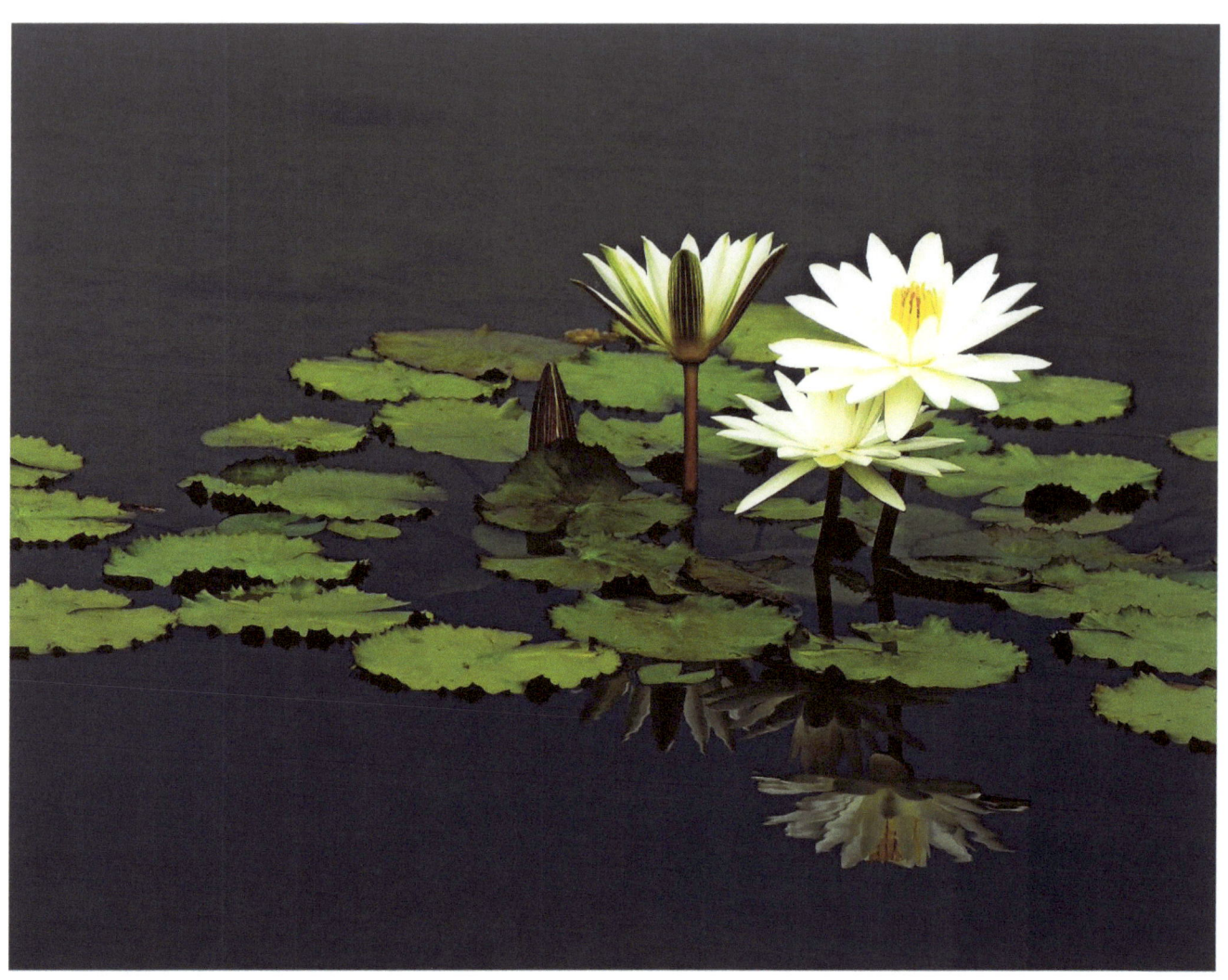

Summer Time

The quiet beauty of a pond is instantly enhanced
by the rounded leaves and flower petals
of the Water Lily floating on the surface.

The beauty of the Water Lily makes the Ozark ponds
even more special this time of year.

My God is the creator, designer and master painter of it all.

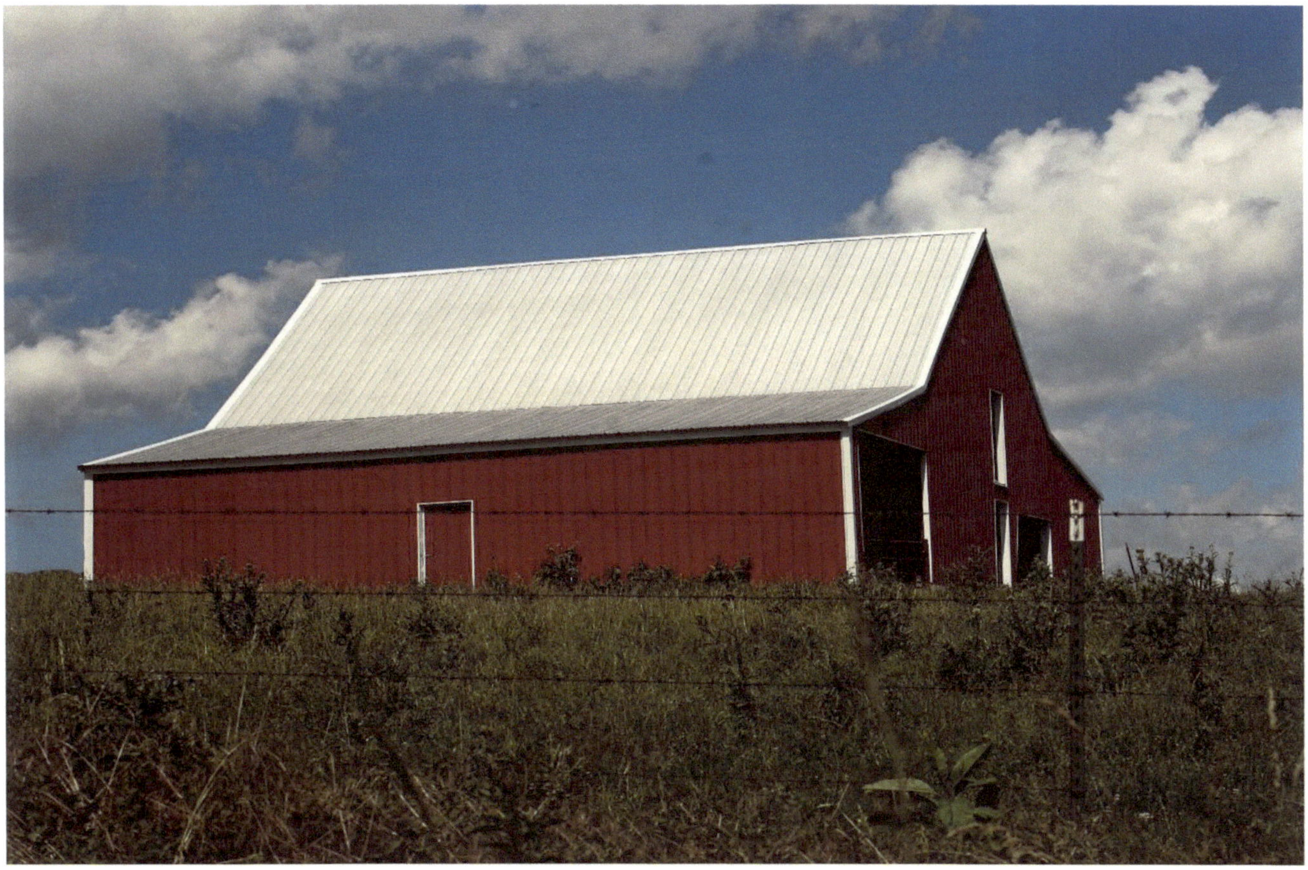

Summer road trip.

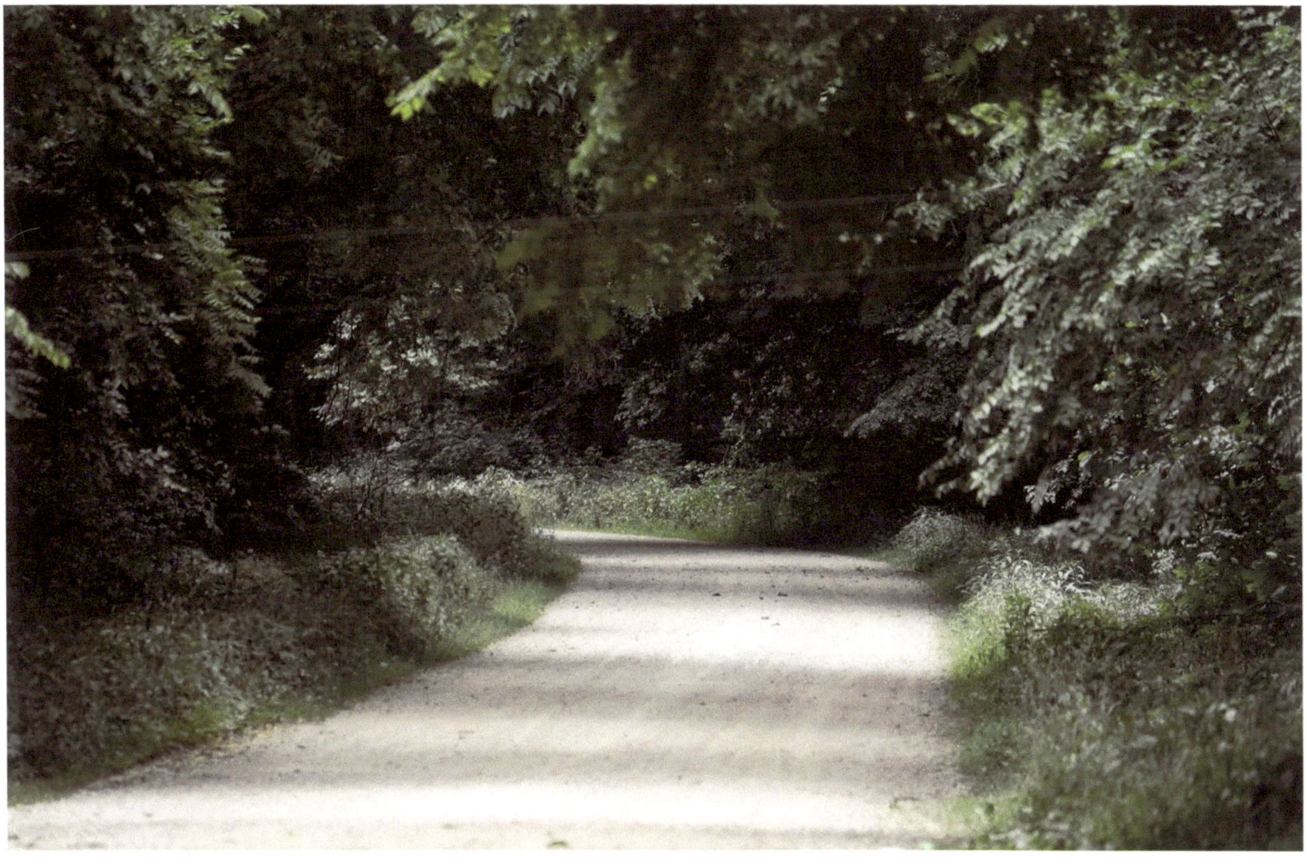

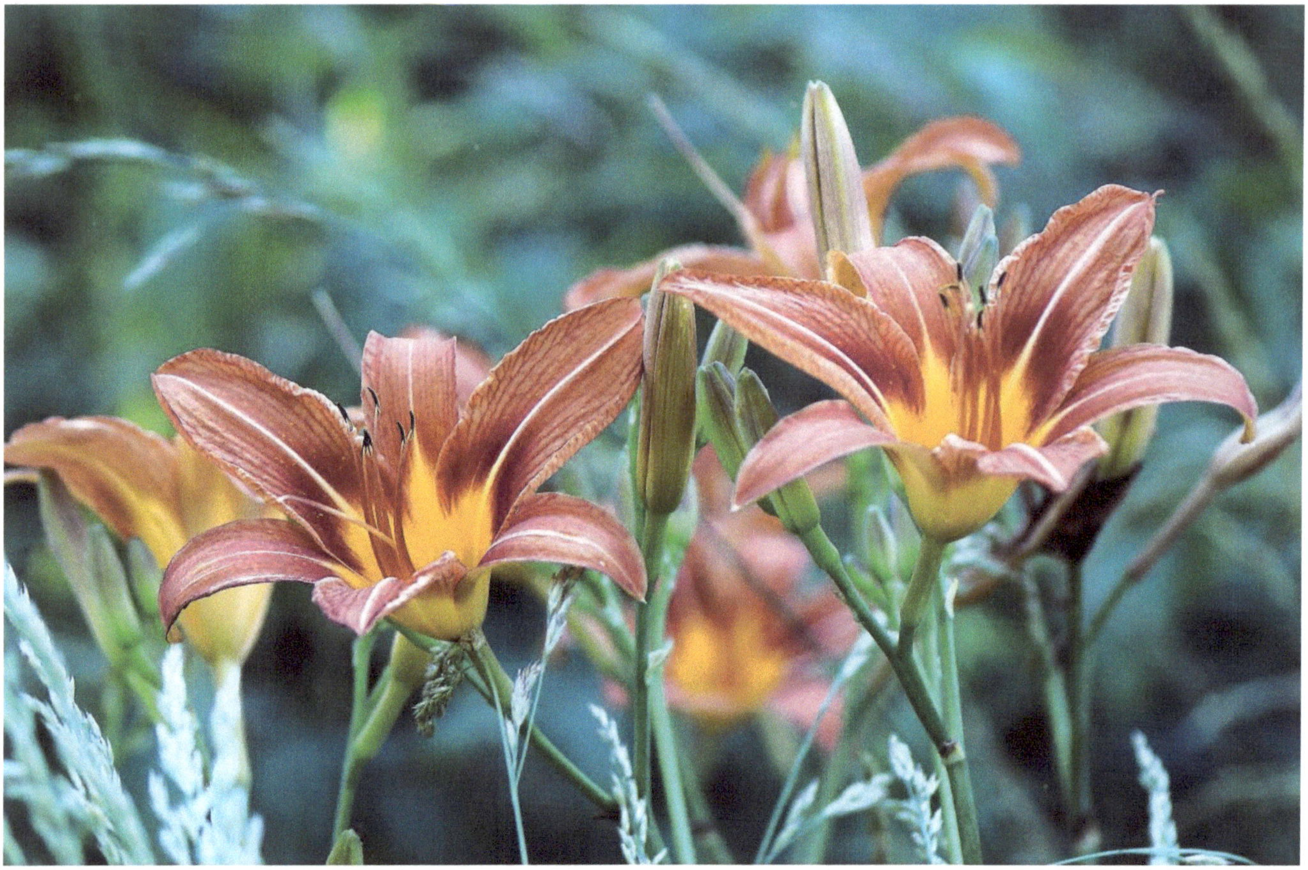

Go outdoors and enjoy nature on a beautiful day.

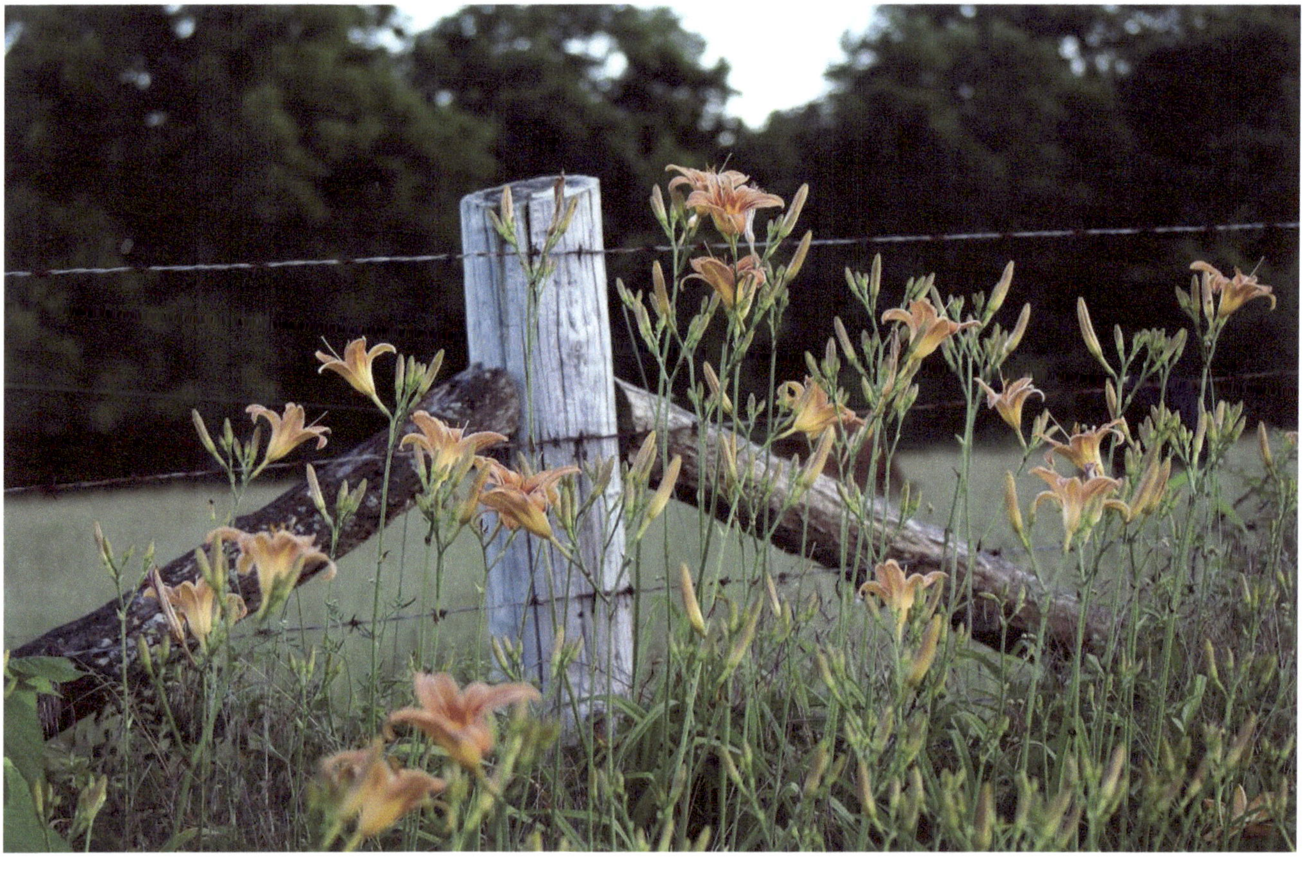

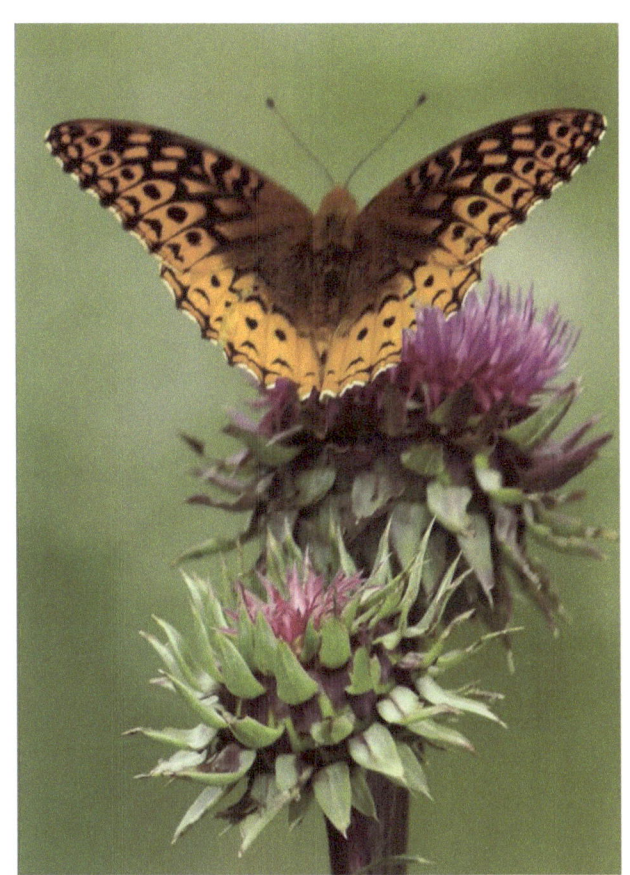 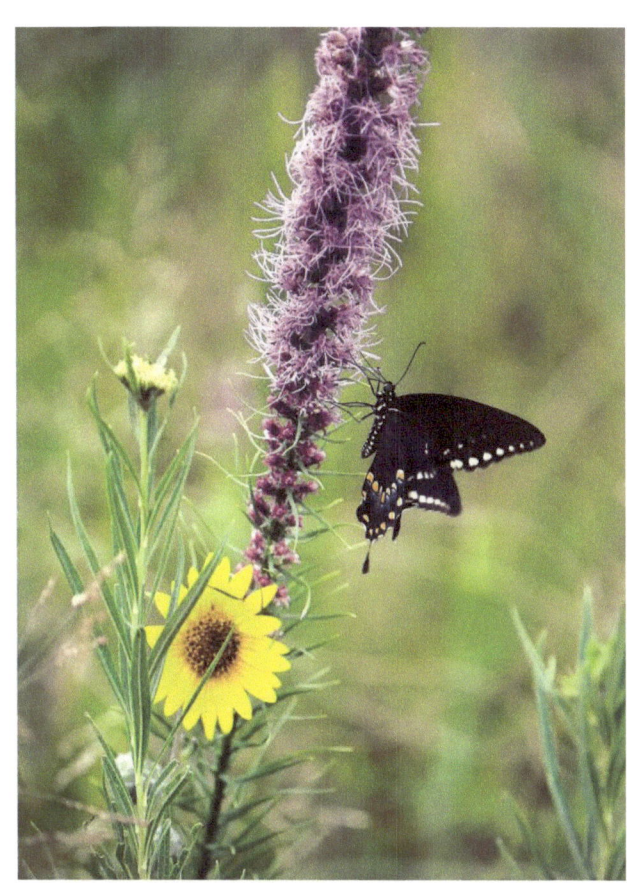

Nature is God's artwork and he is the master painter of all.

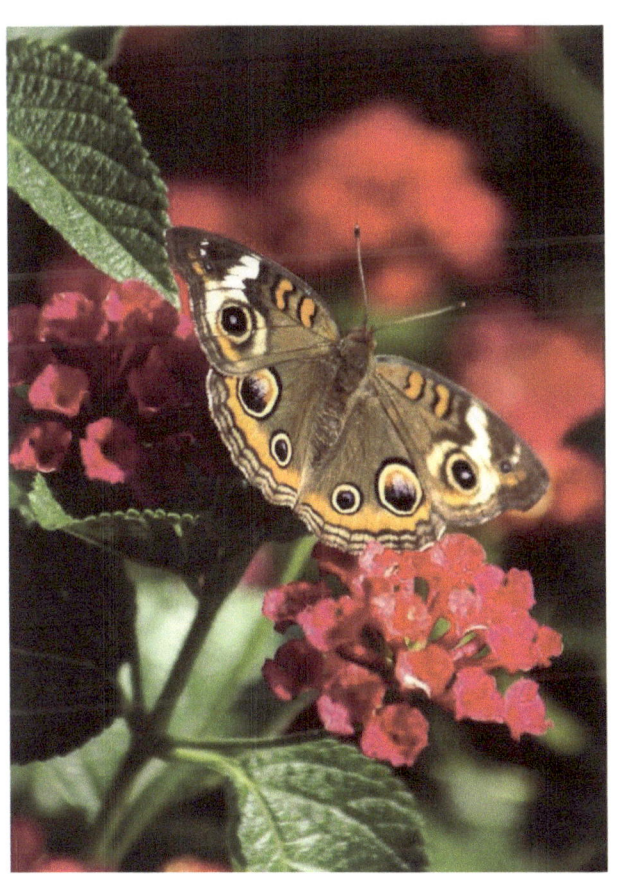 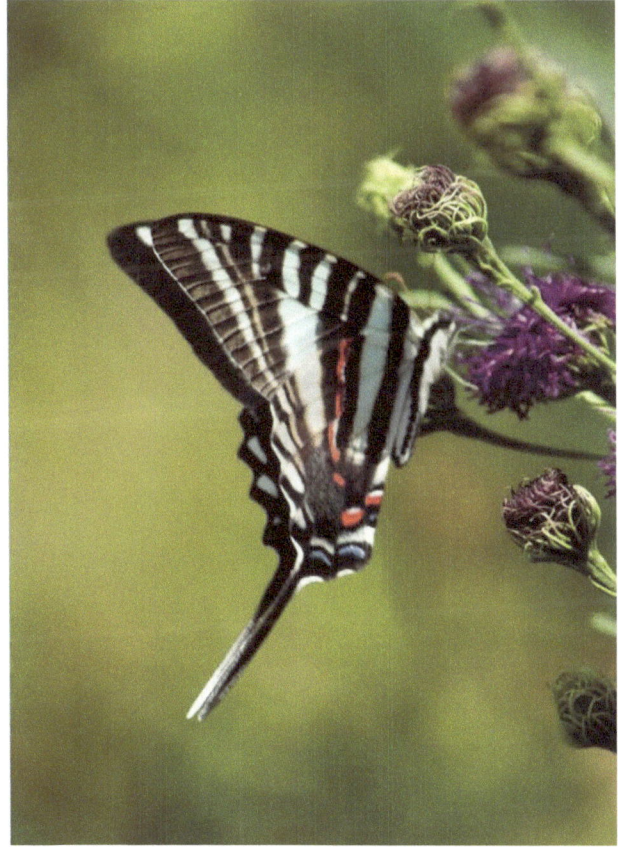

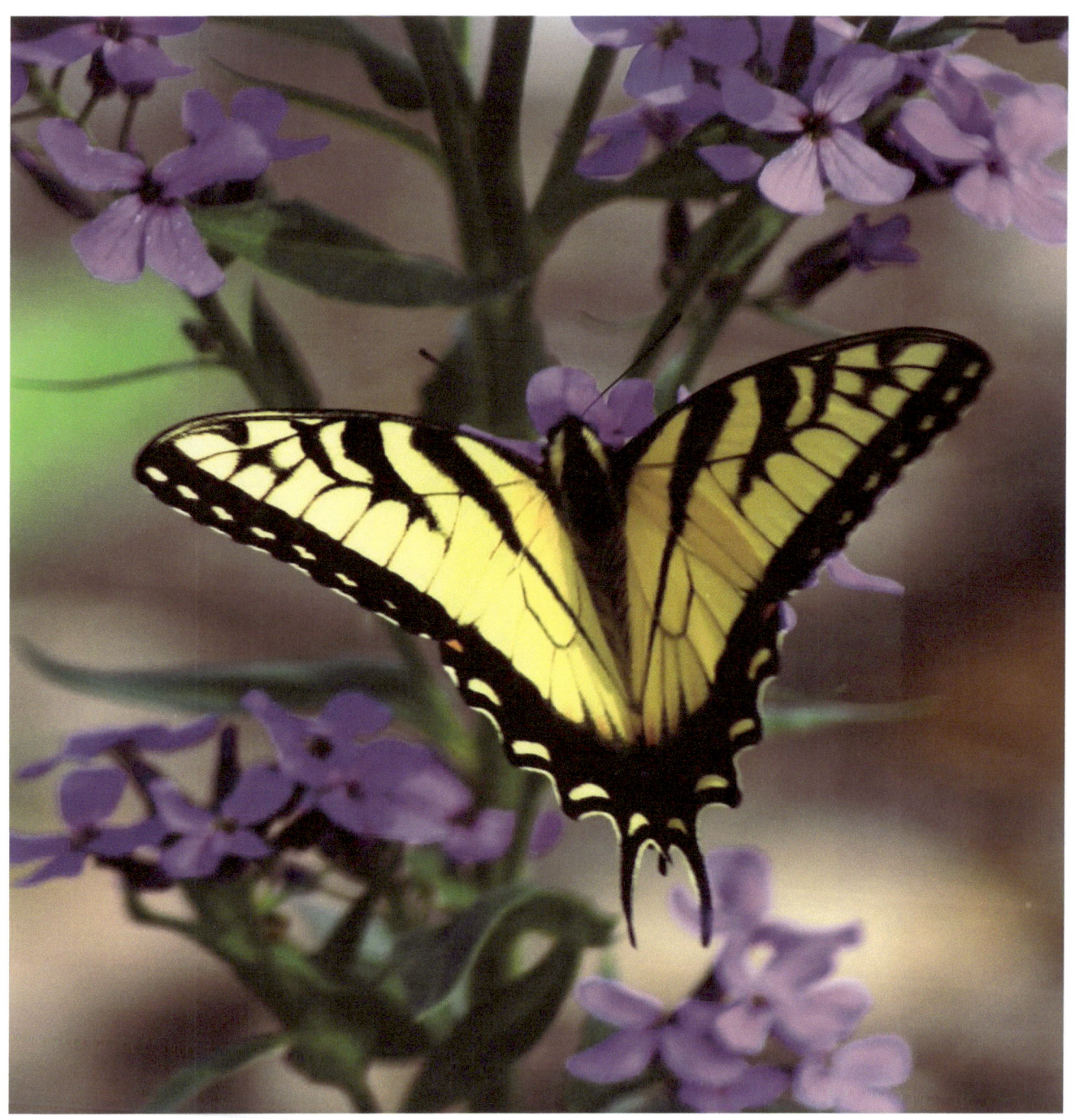

It is a bright sunshine day and we are out for a ride in country
(with camera in hand),
witnessing the beauty of many different types of butterflies,
gracefully gliding though the air with their colors ever so bright.

They do not stay very long in one place, but what a sight to see.

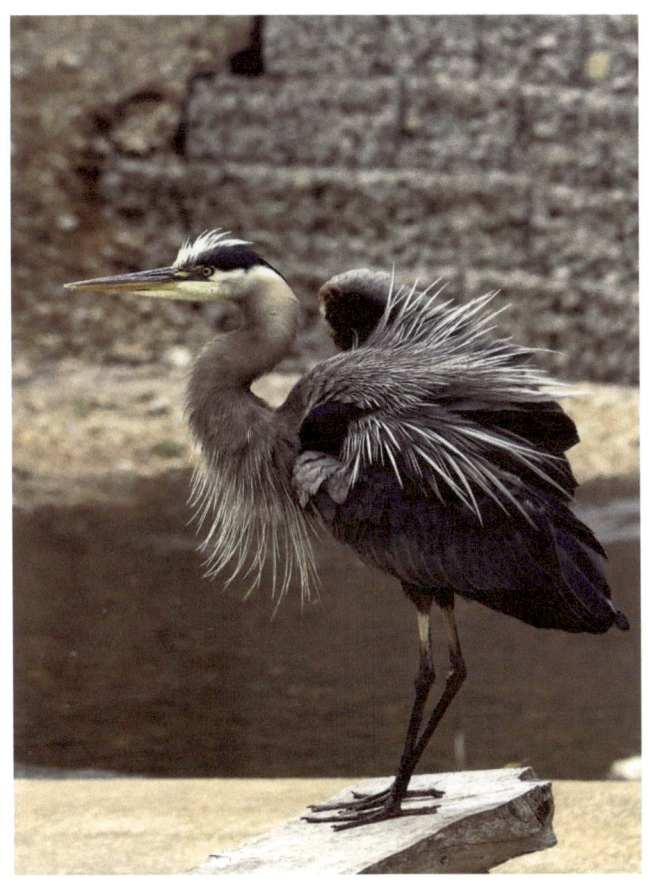 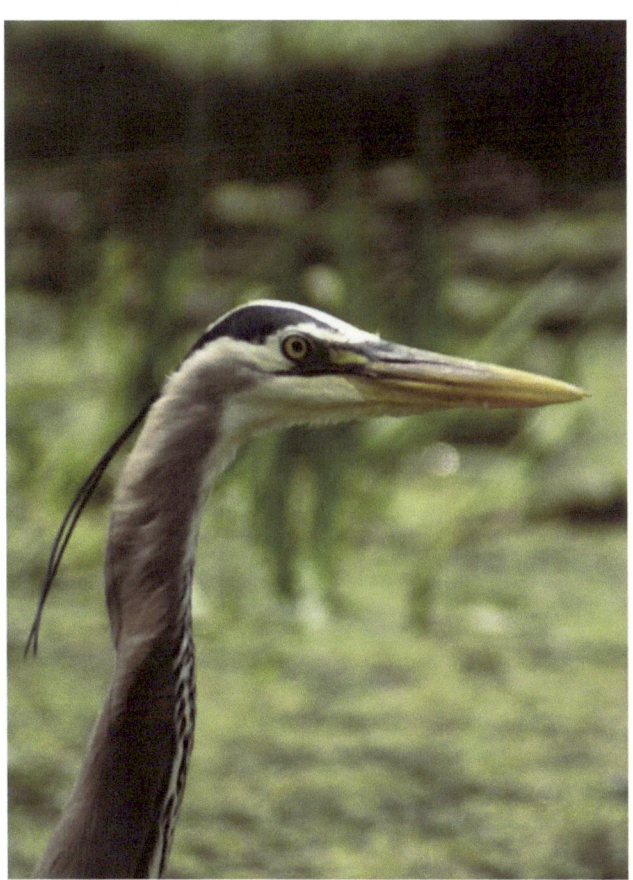

Nature is full of surprises.

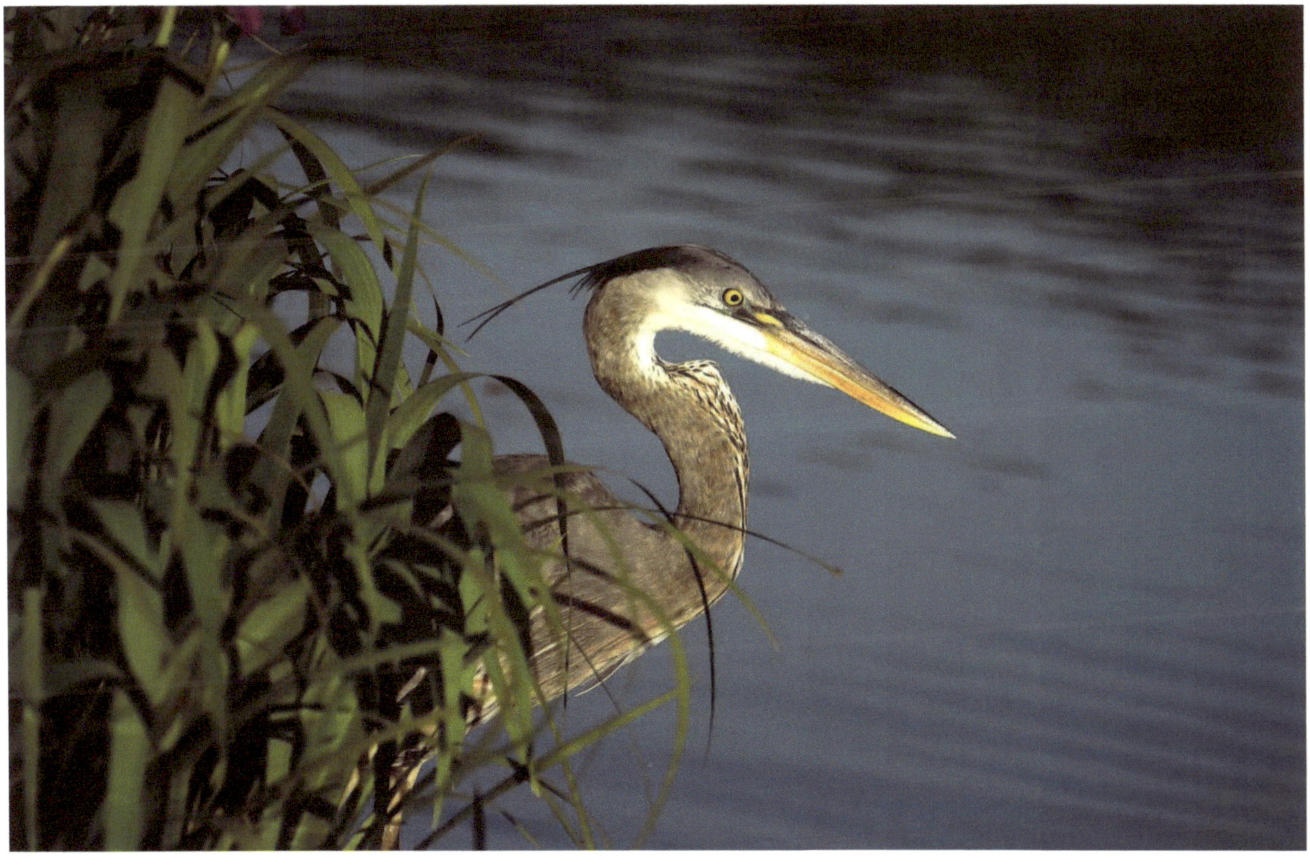

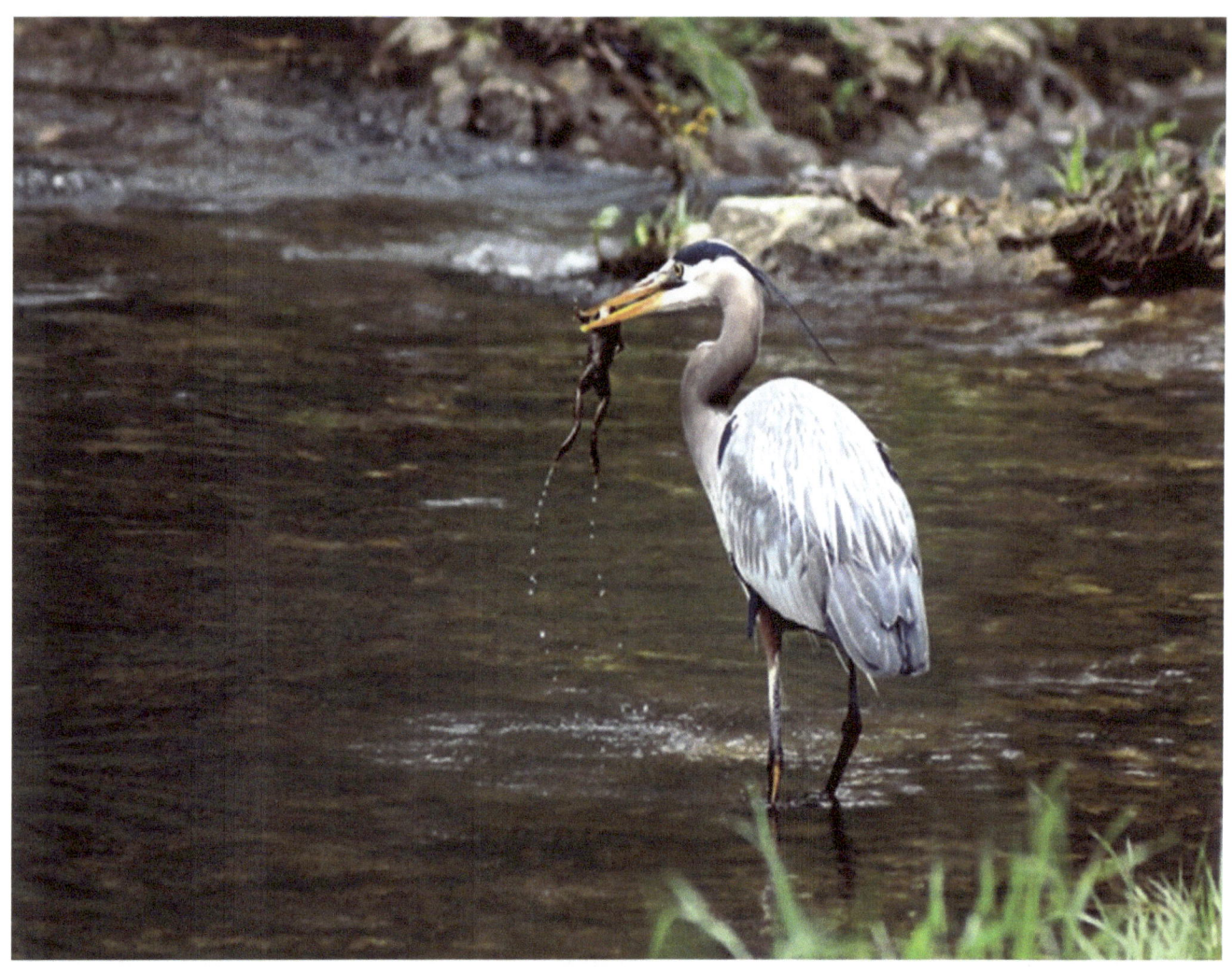

Lunch Time

It was Summer time and we were out on a photo shoot.
Crossed a bridge over a creek and spotted the Blue Herring.
It soon took flight, flew over, and landed on the other side.
Already had the window down and ready

"click" "I got the shot - Frog not so lucky."

What a wonderful world God has created.

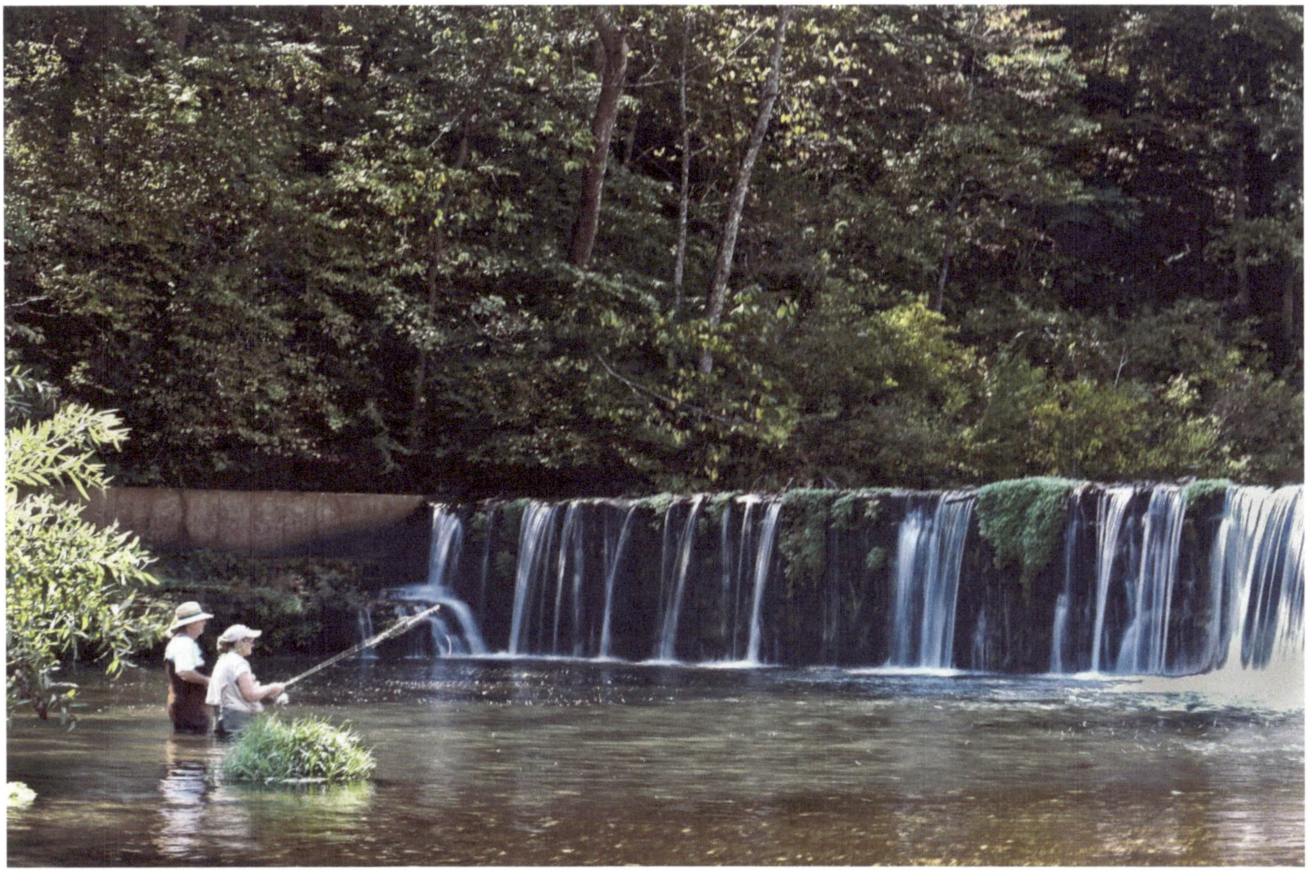

Let's go fishing!

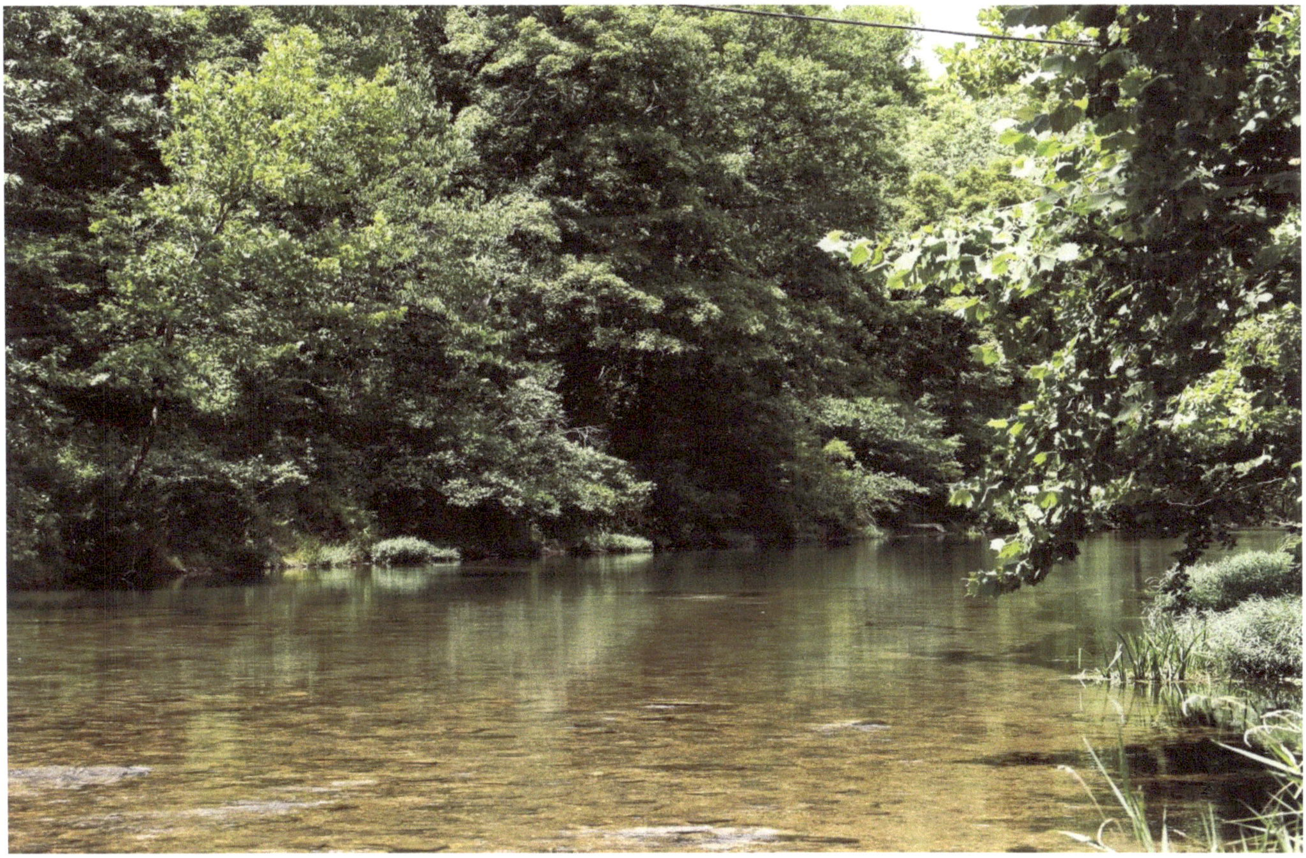

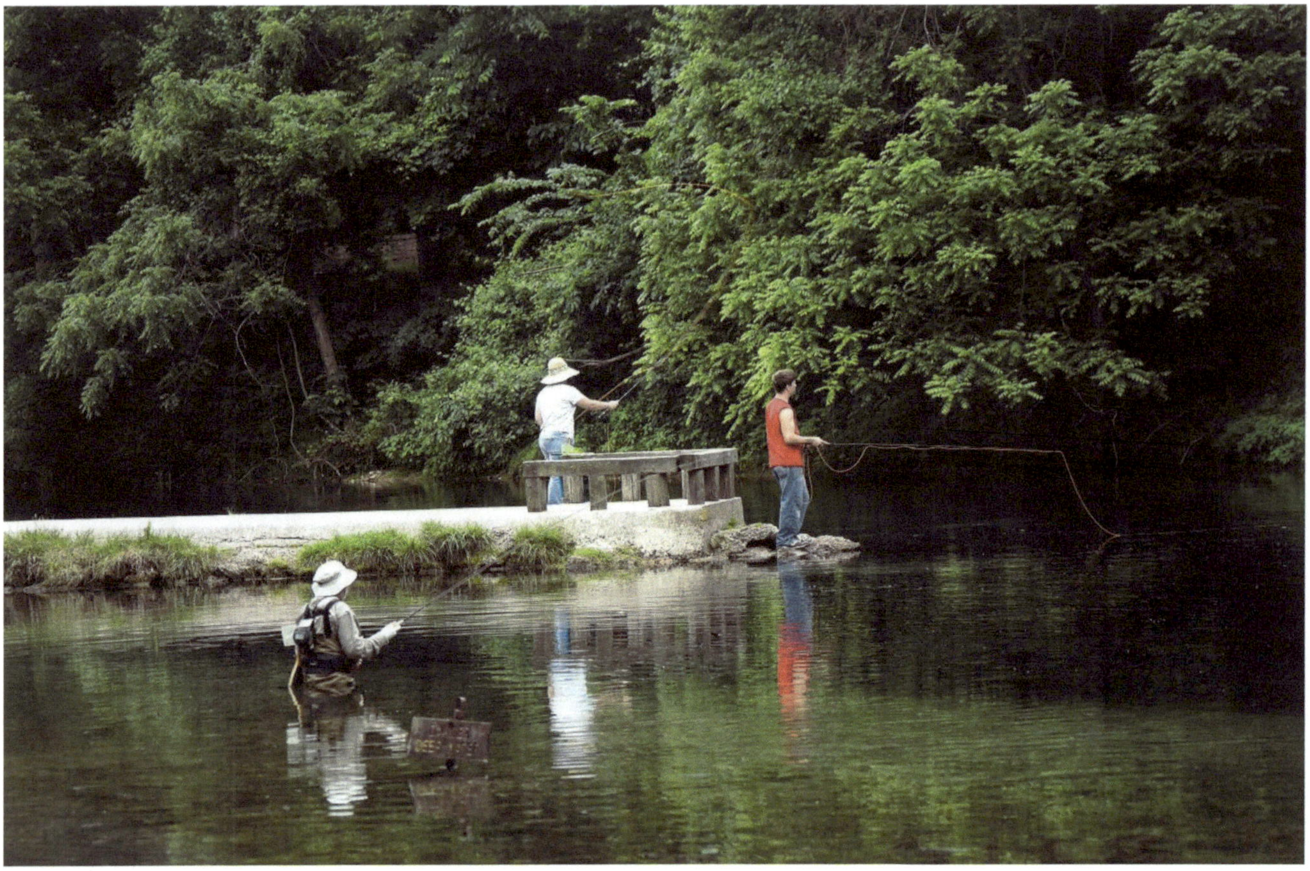

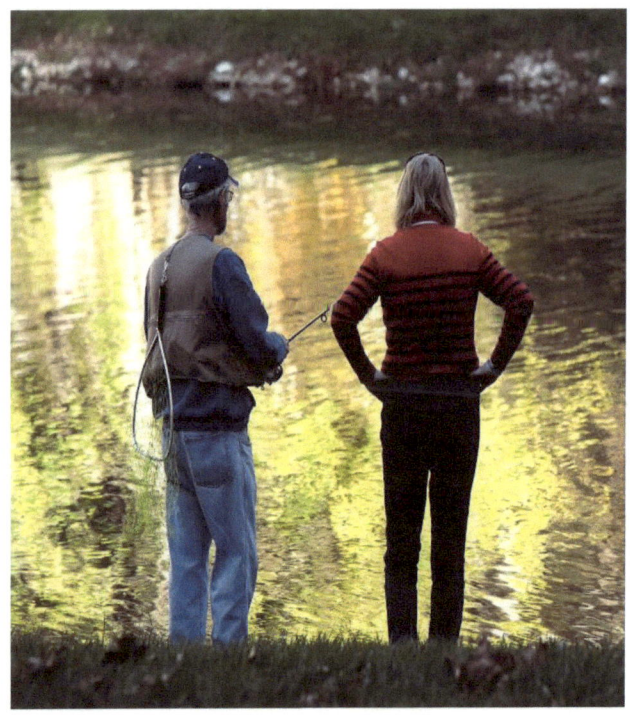

On our road trips, we often stop to take photos from the van along the side of the road.

Many of the roads are like a roller coaster ride, dips and sharp turns. I always have camera ready on the lookout for the next photo.

On a cool afternoon in the Summer, it is a good time to go fishing, in the rivers or ponds in the Ozark.

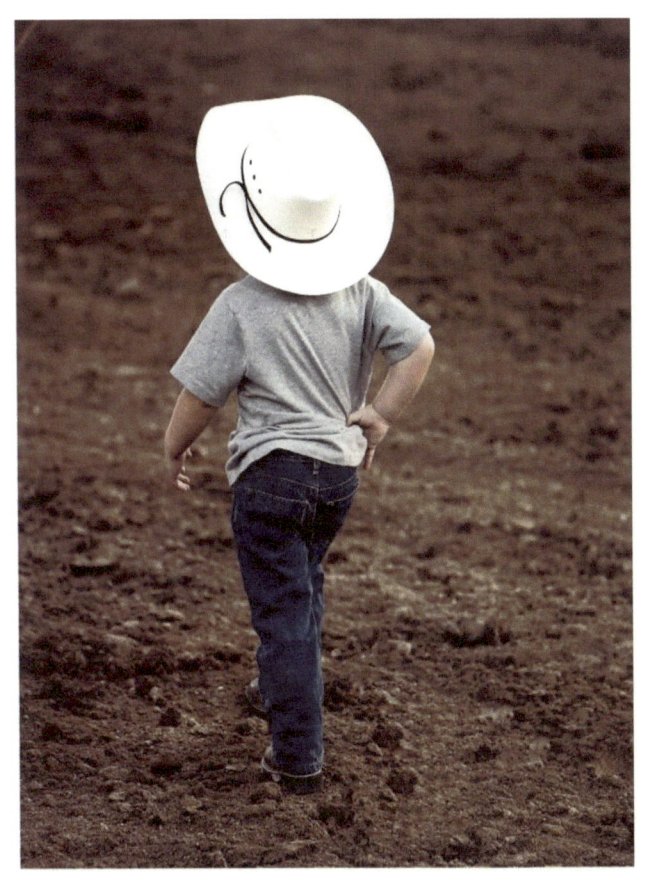
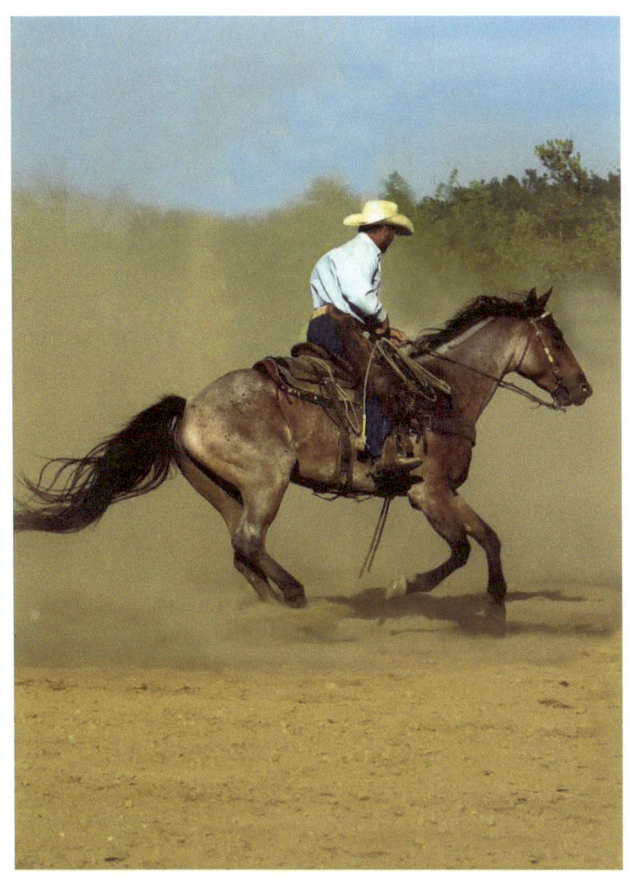

Ride'em Cowboy!

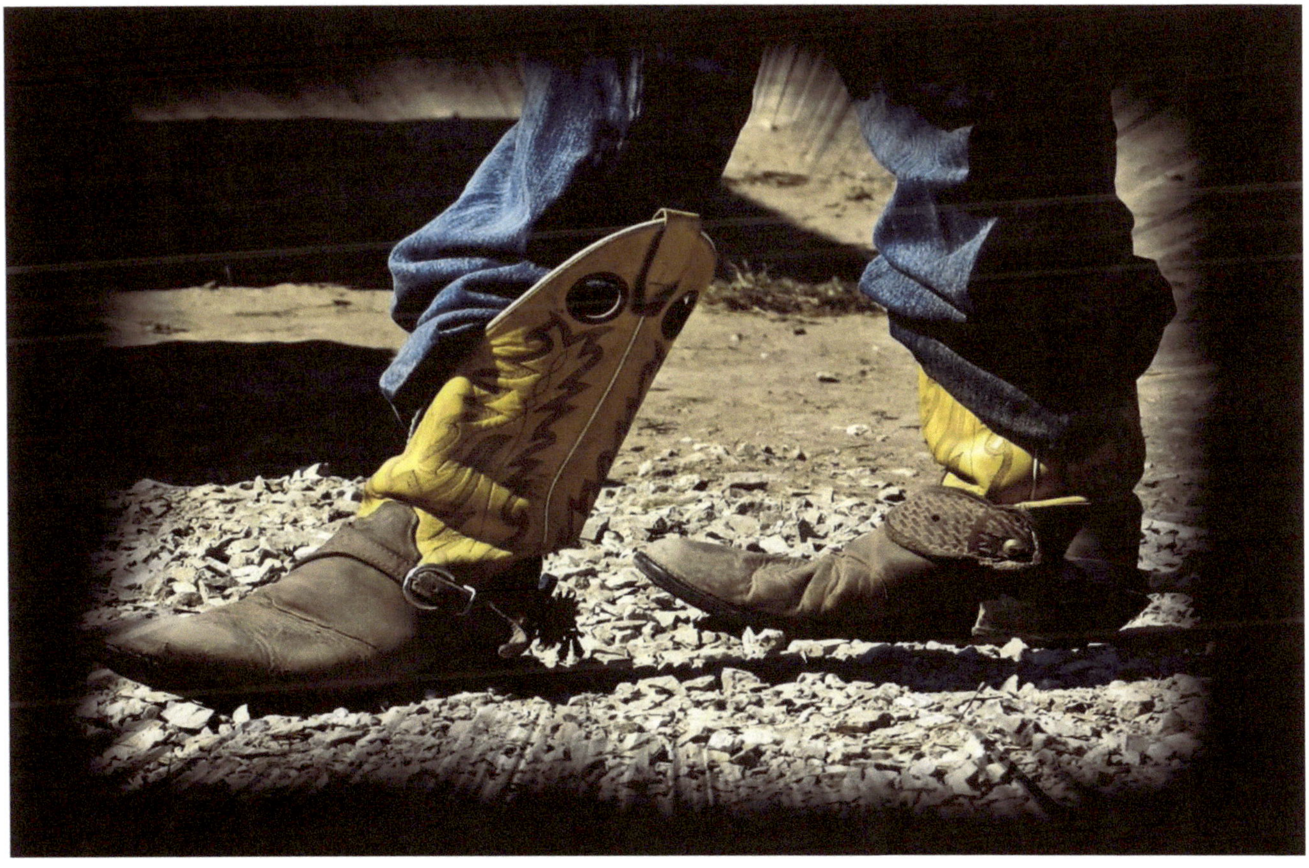

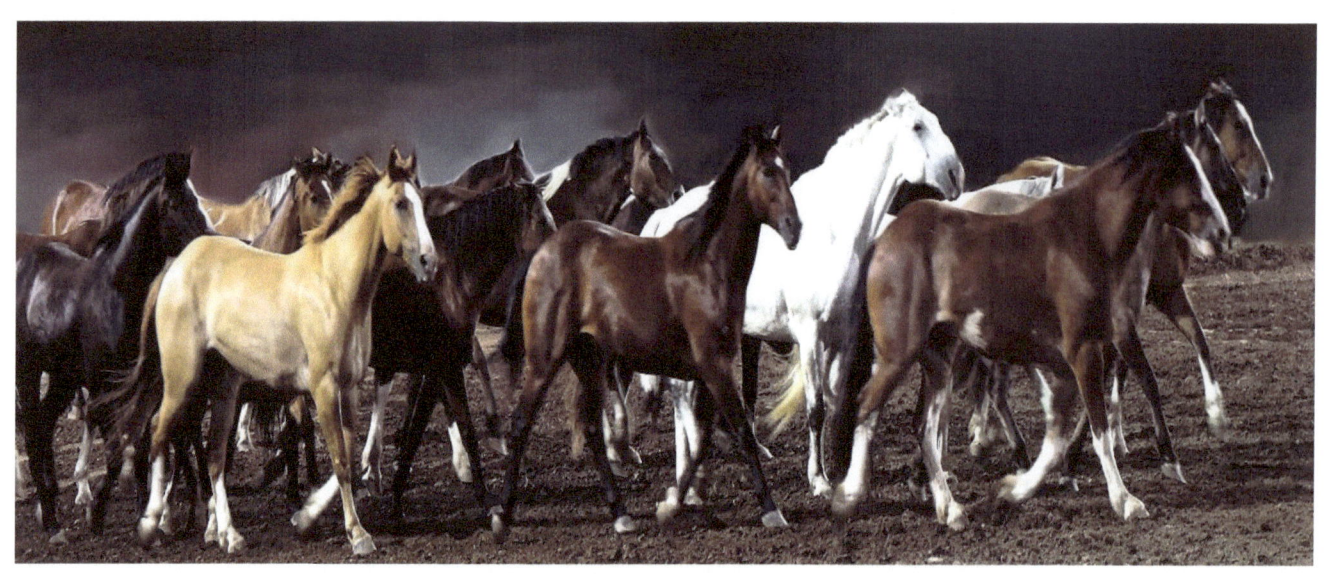

When going out in the country on a photoshoot,
you go through many small towns. Sometimes they
will have a rodeo, even in the hot Summer heat.
Lot of action, tricky to capture.

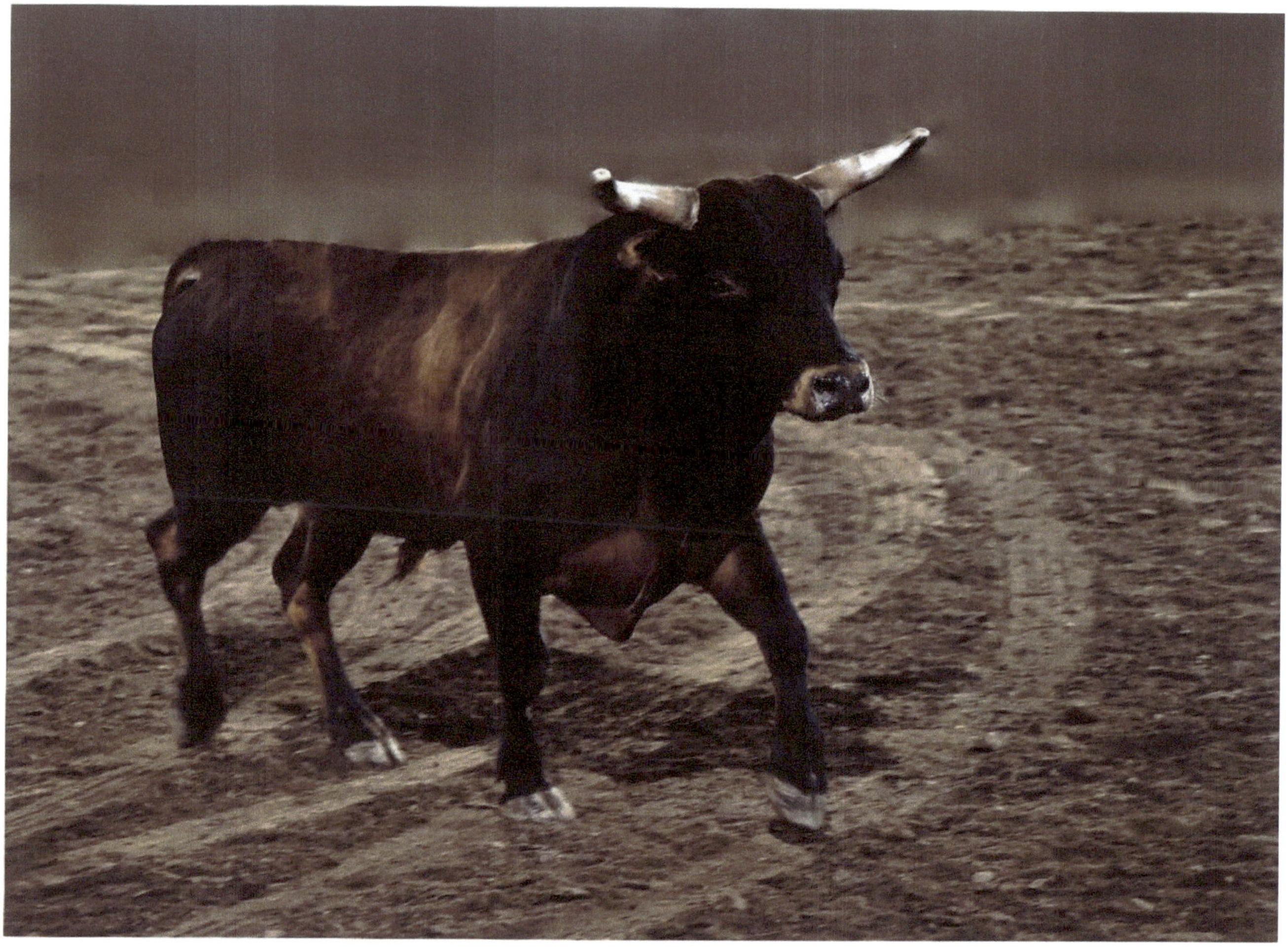

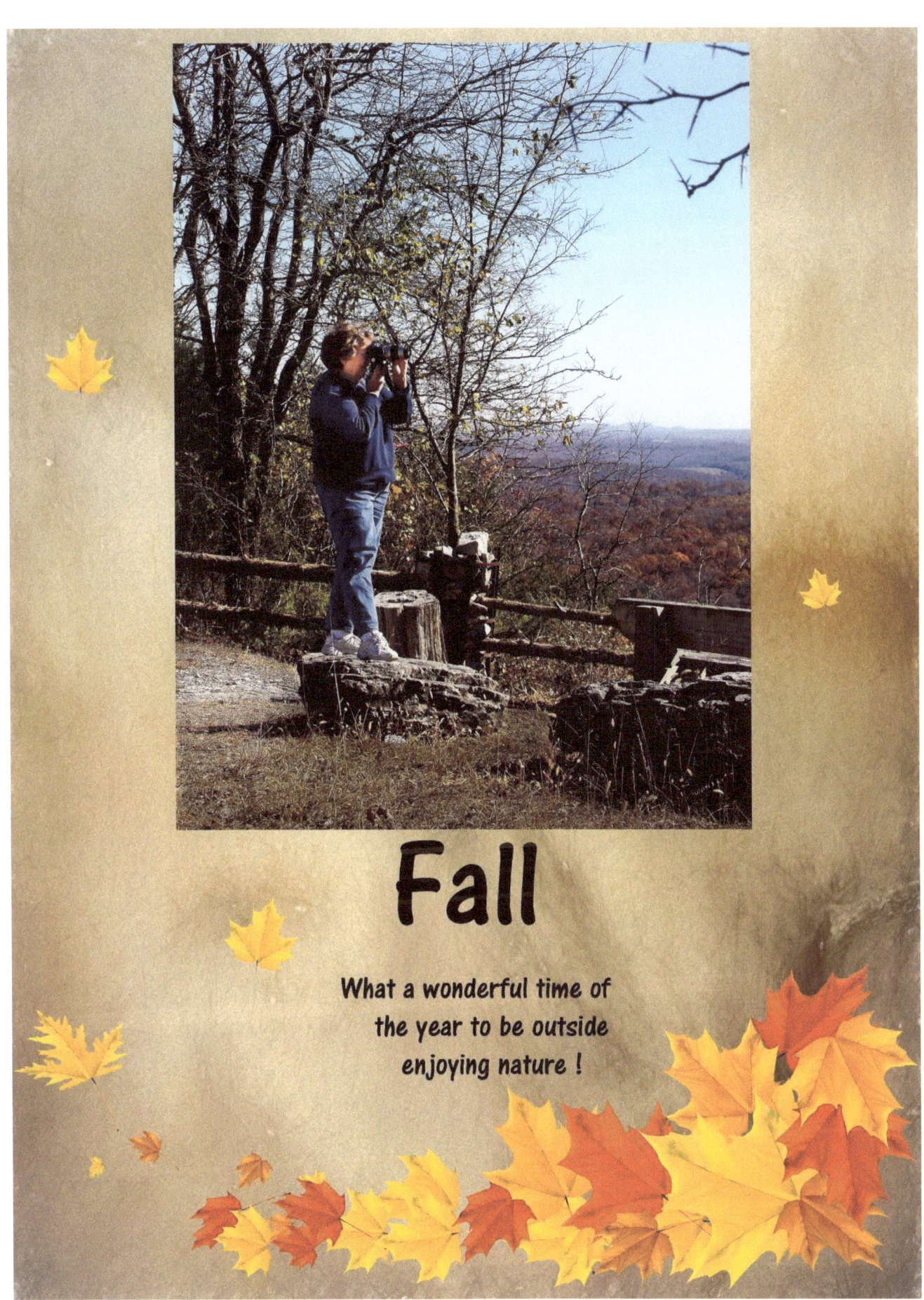

Fall

What a wonderful time of the year to be outside enjoying nature!

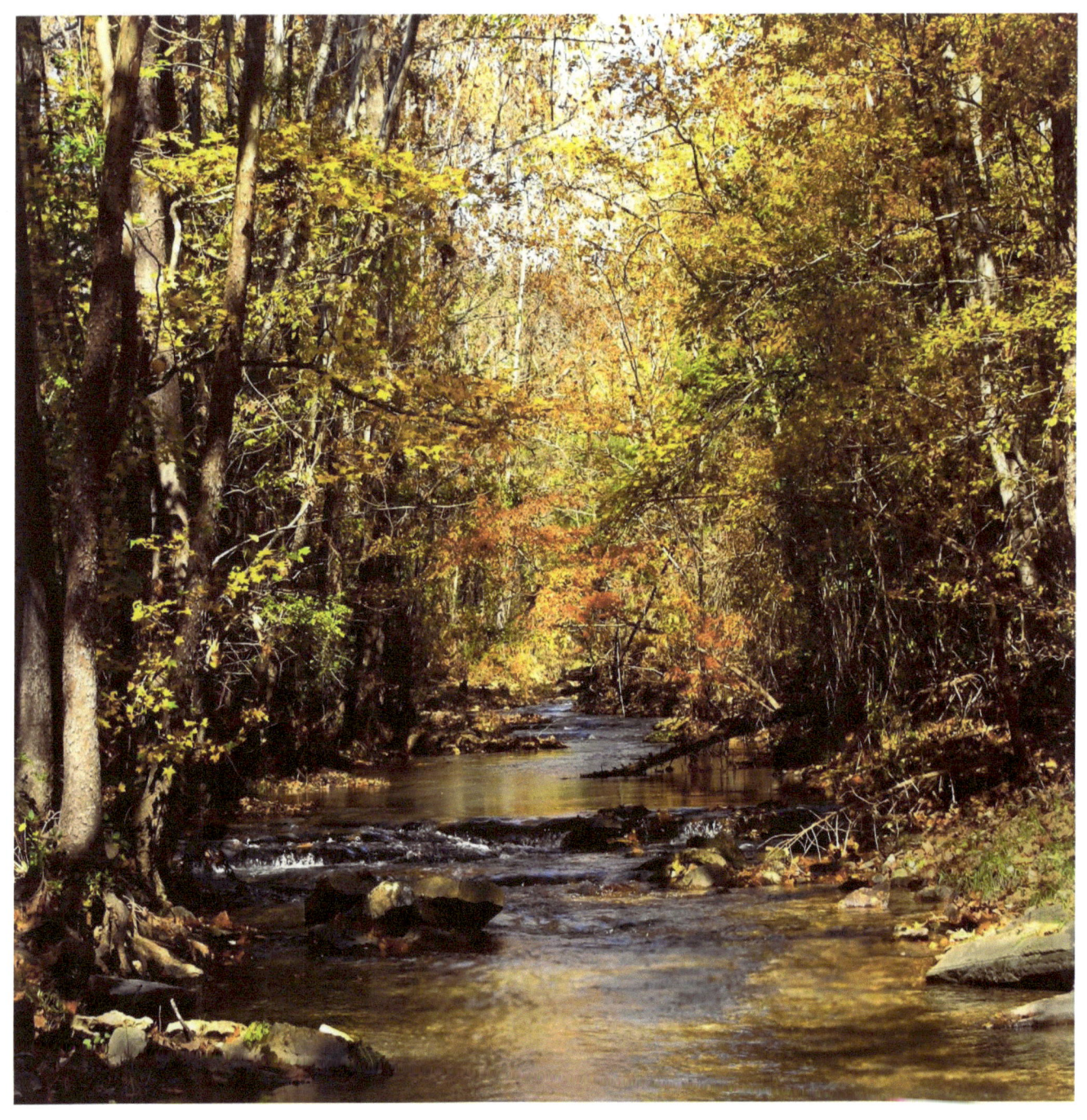

Fall is a great time of the year.

In the Fall, God is a lavish master painter,
He loves the vibrant red, orange, gold, and rustic brown.
He painted the leaves in all the trees
we saw along the way.

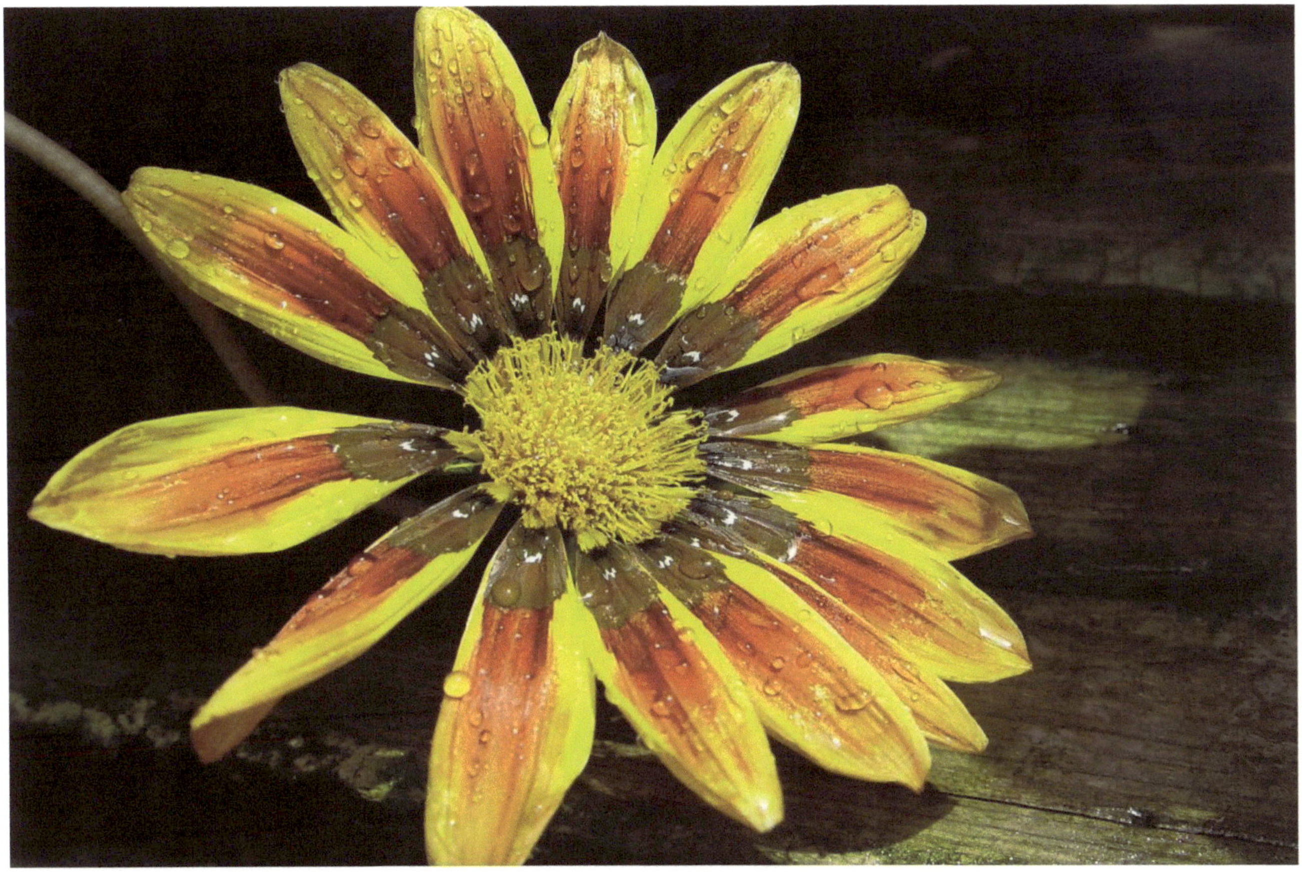

Join me on a adventure this bright sunshiny day.

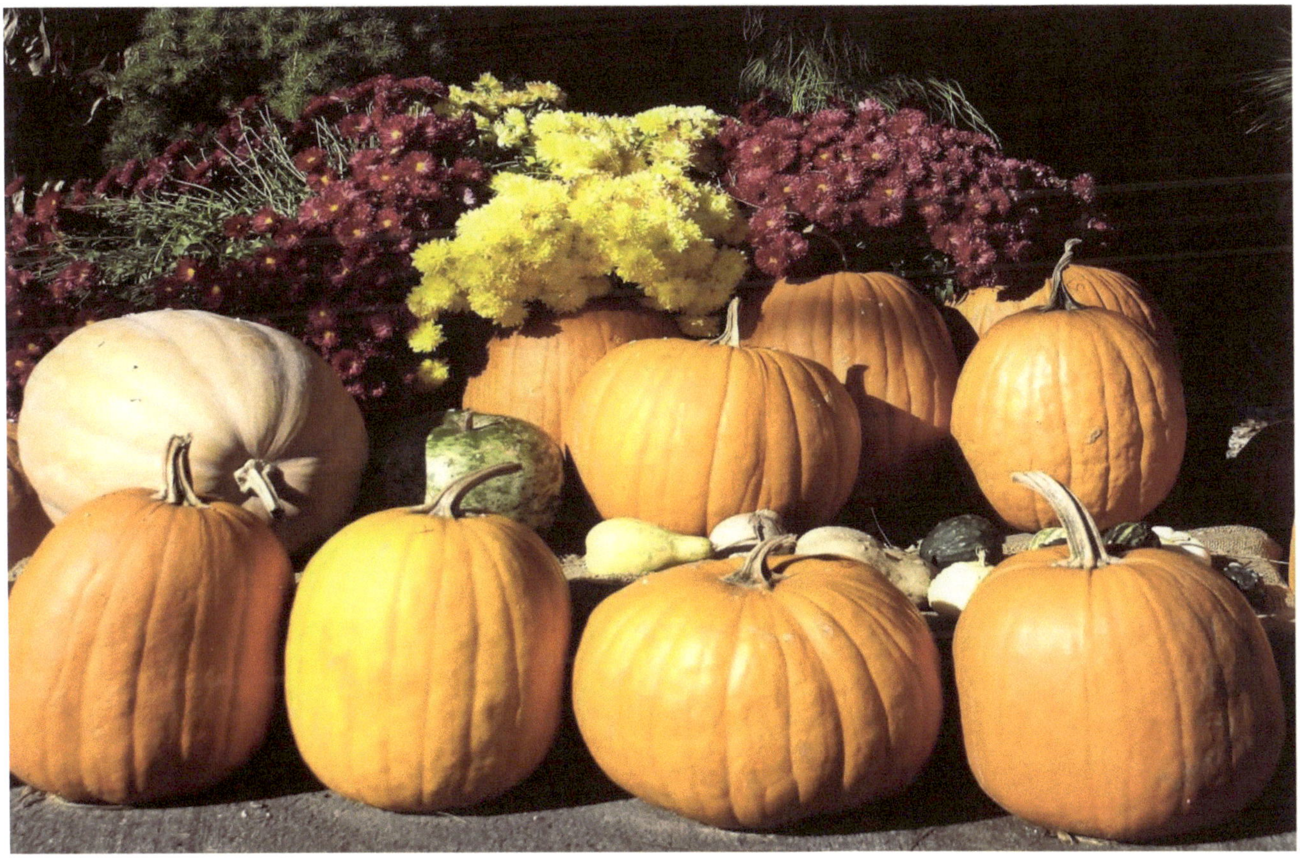

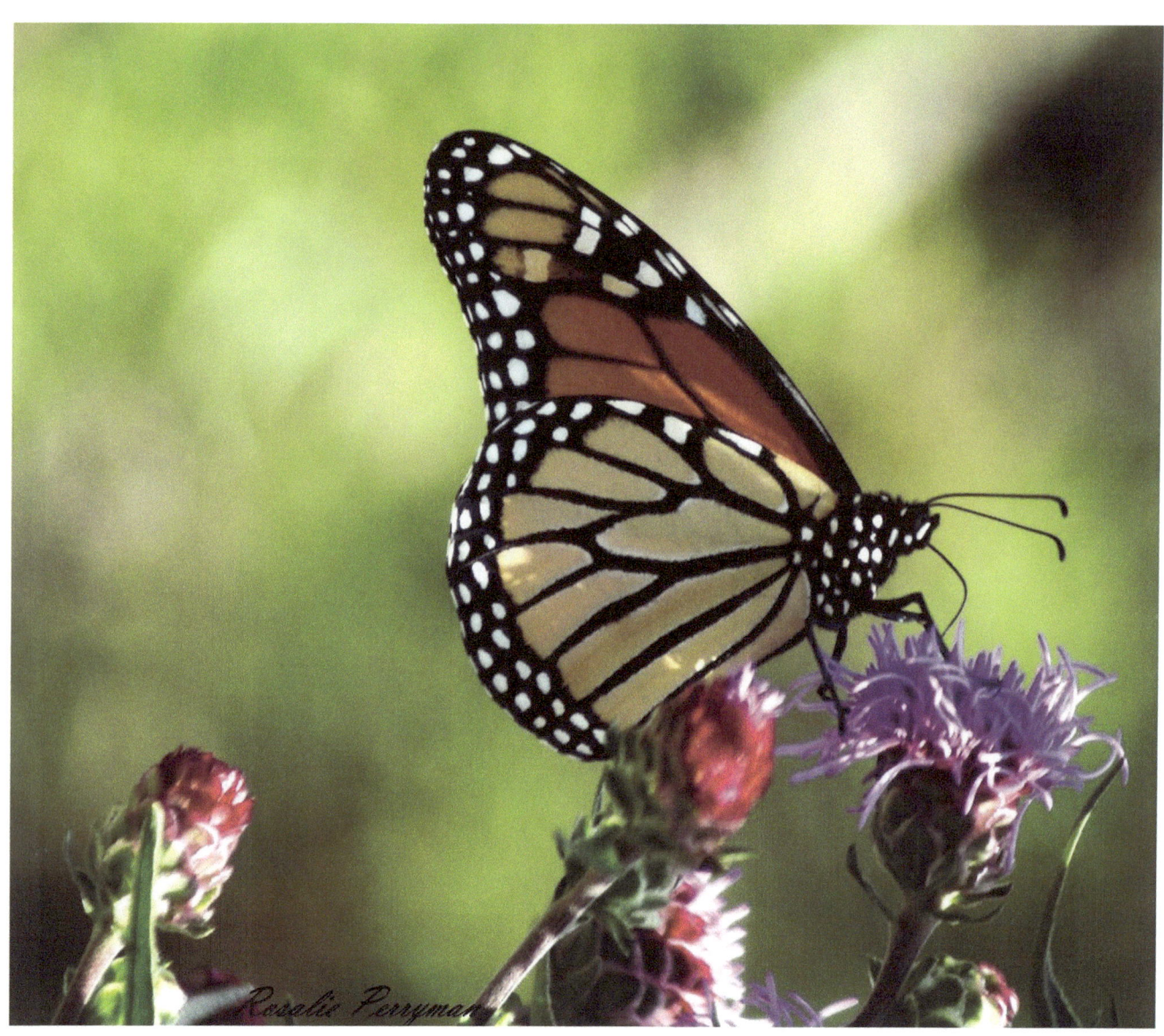

While traveling down many old country crooked, winding, dusty roads, over the hills and valleys, I have seen butterflies everywhere.
They seem to not notice me as they dance and flitter passing by.

Patience is needed when taking photos of butterflies.
I always want to see what is around the next corner.
As you can see, God has designed glorious butterflies.

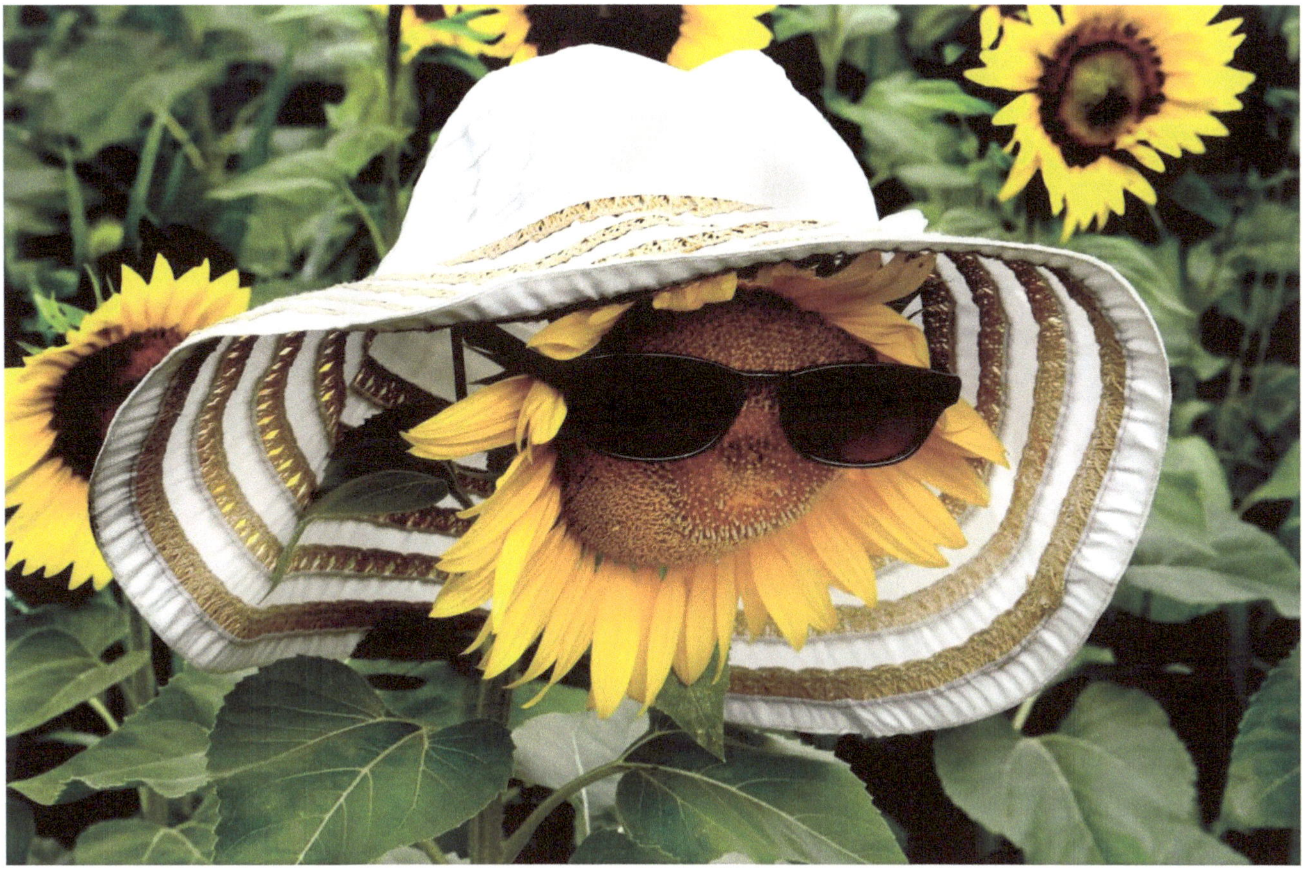

Thank you God for another good day.

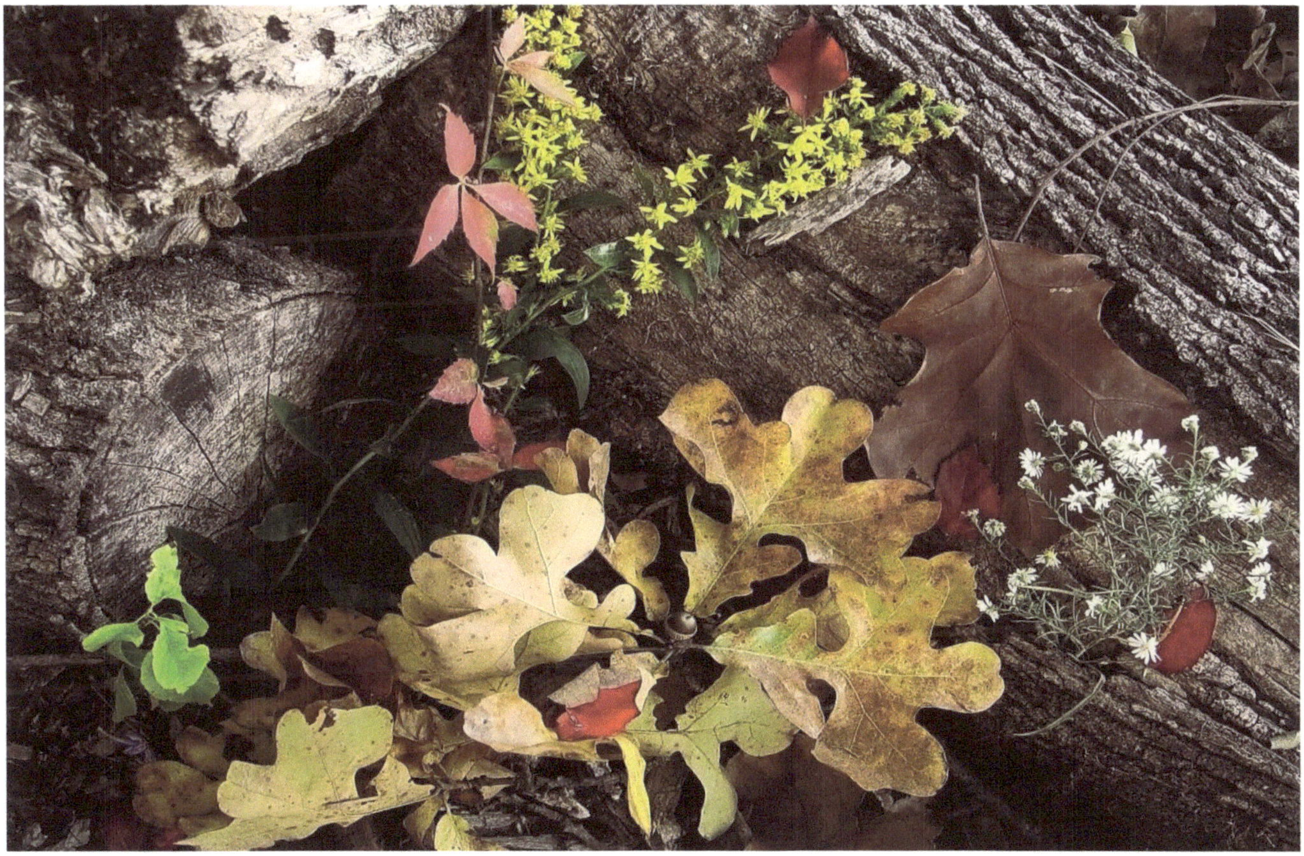

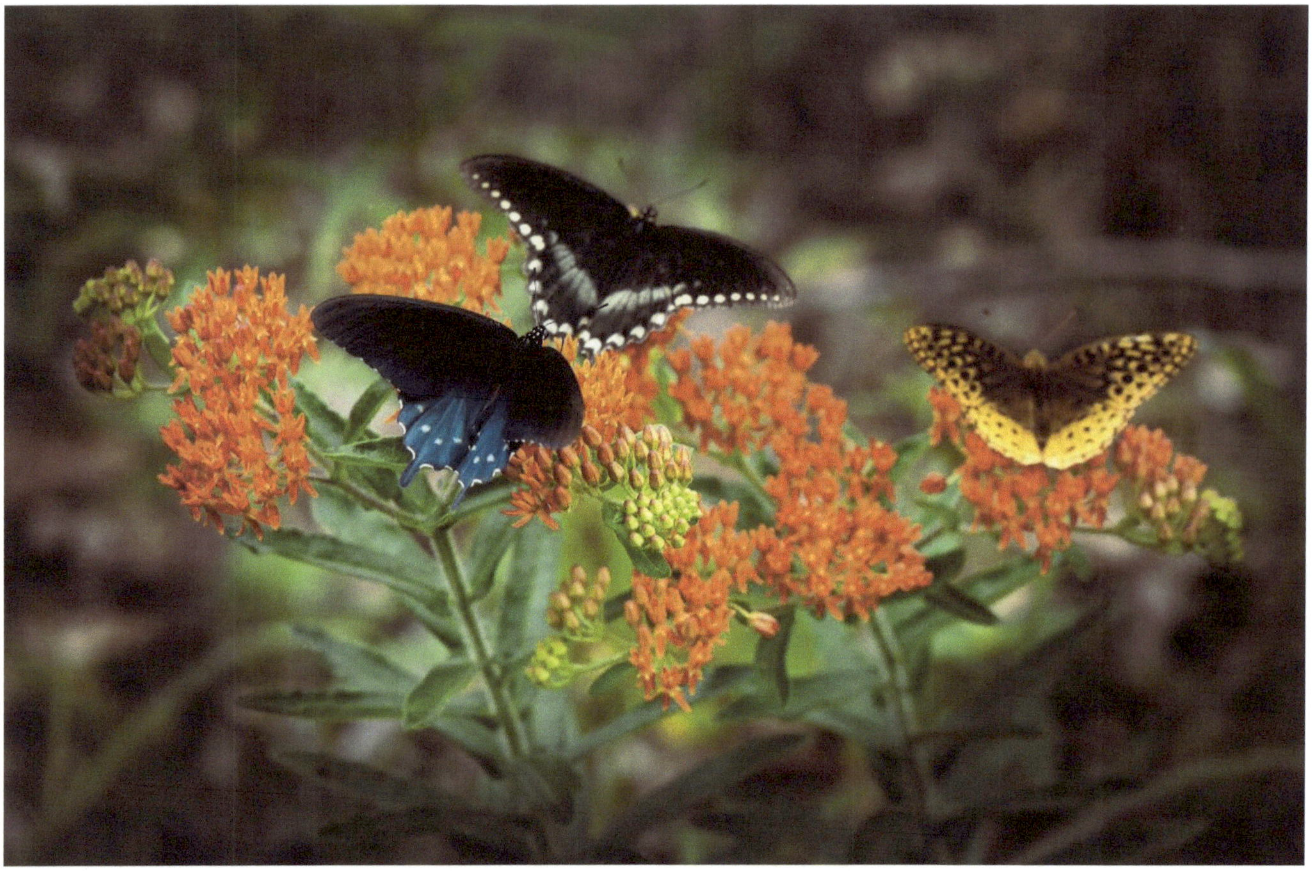

Being in the right place at the right time.

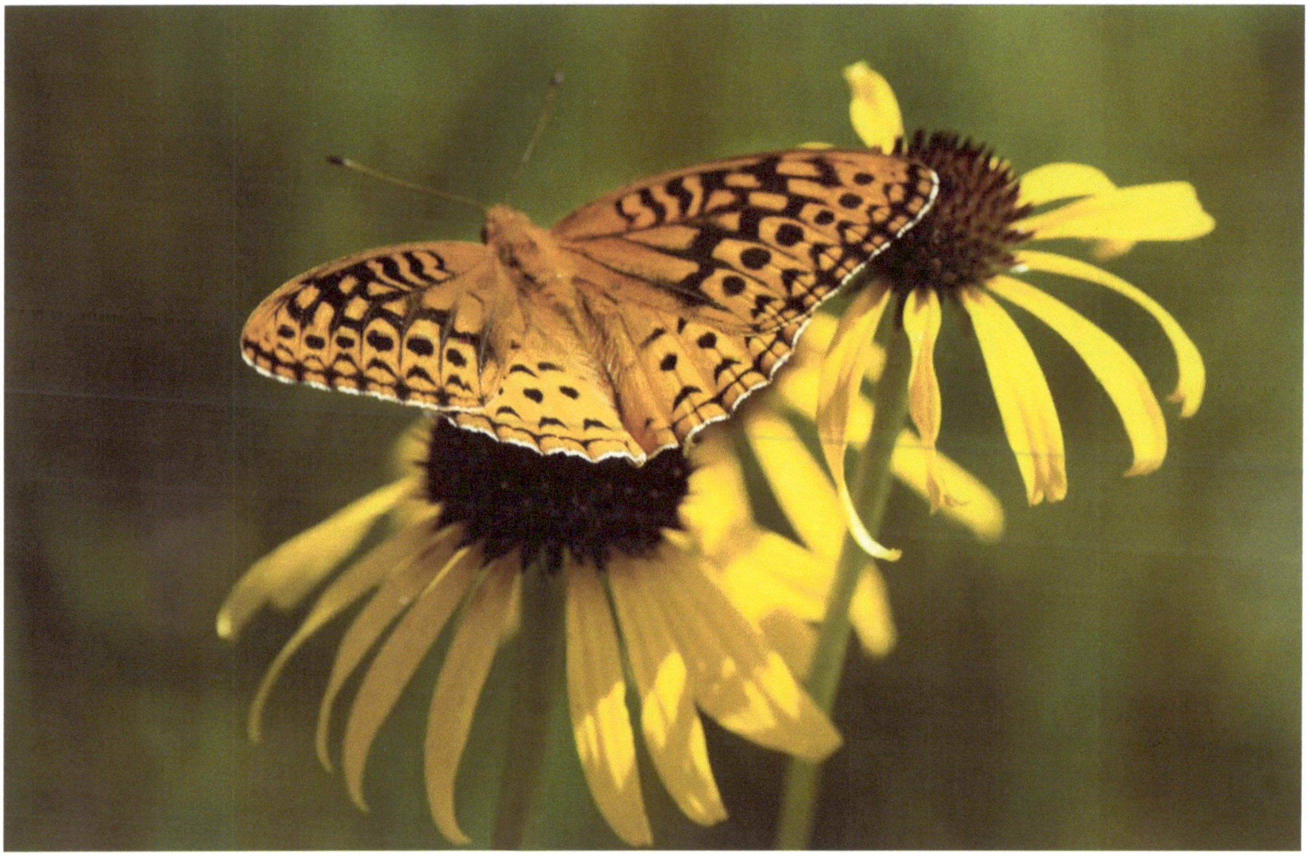

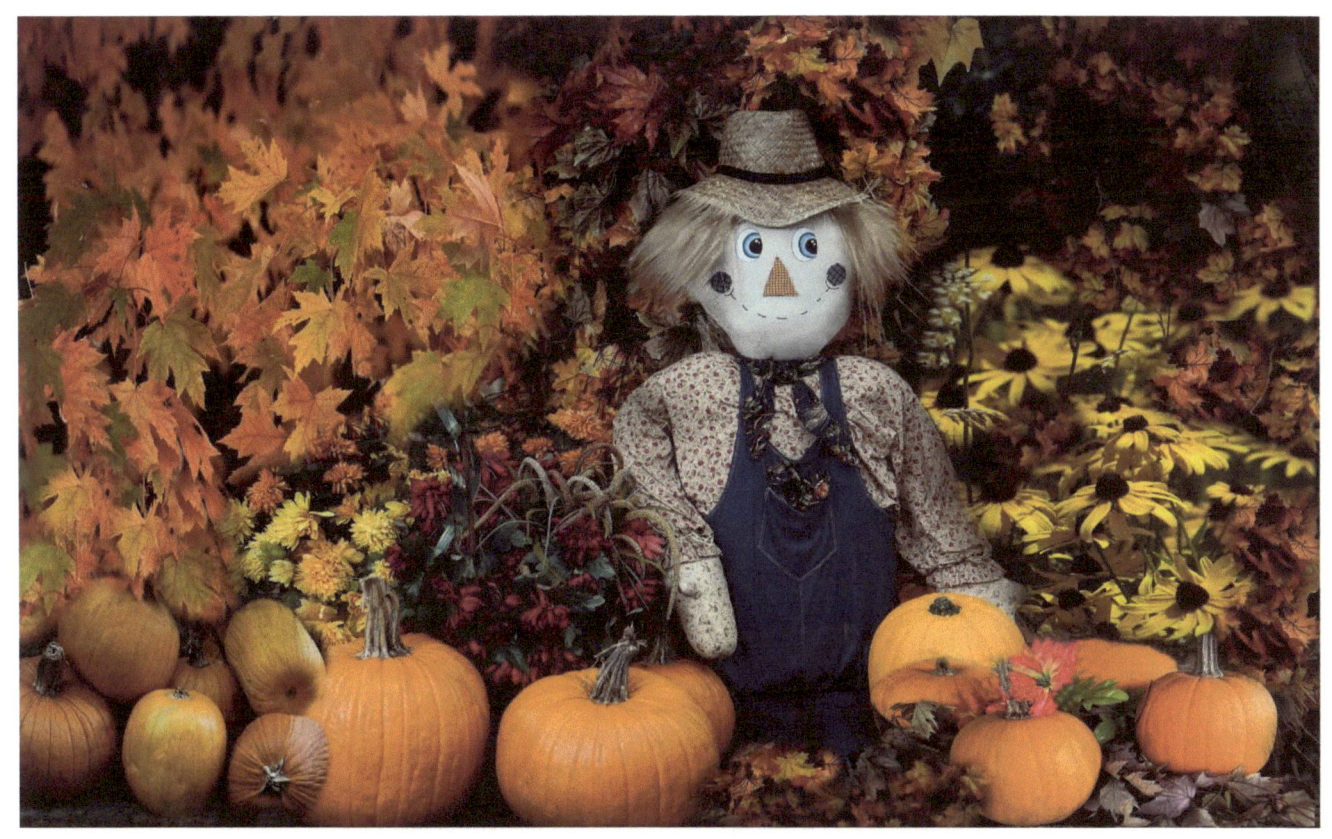

Along the way, the hills were splashed
with gold and red for everyone to see.

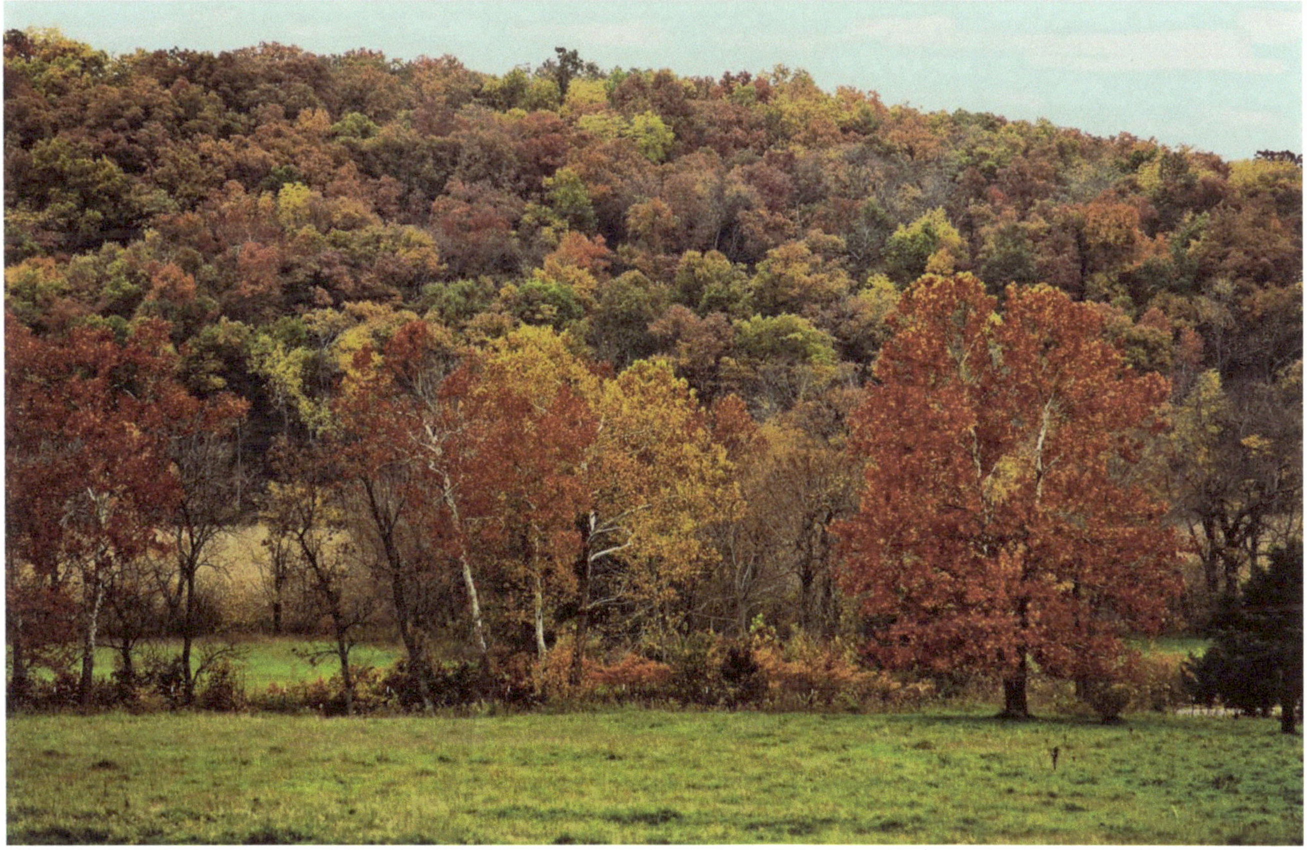

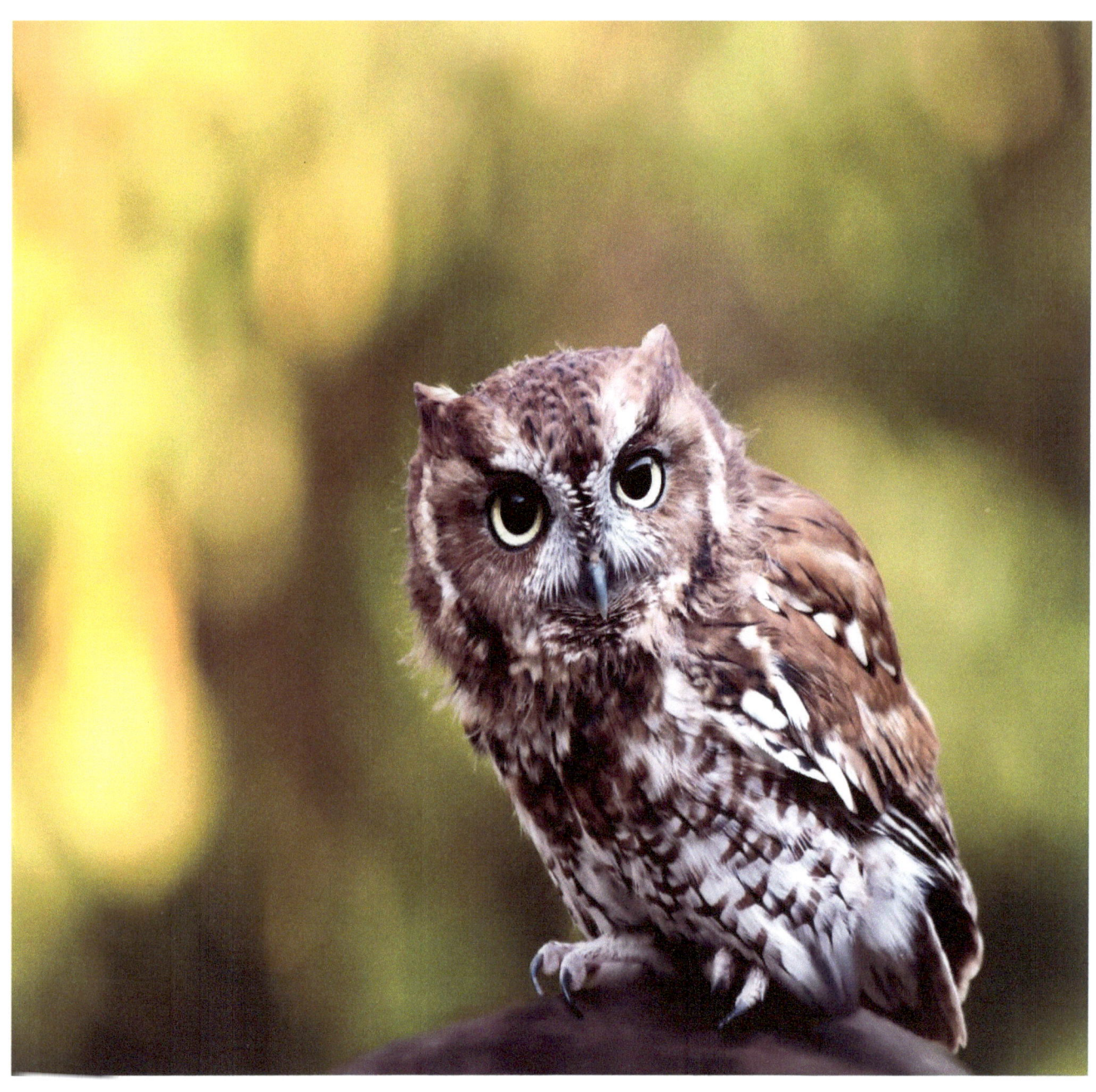

God as the master painter has a wealth of colors to choose from. Sometimes the right colors are needed to blend in or stand out.

On a crisp Autumn windy day as the sun was going down,
spotted this owl and was able to get the photo.
Then he was gone!

Sumac brightens up the Fall colors along the back country roads.

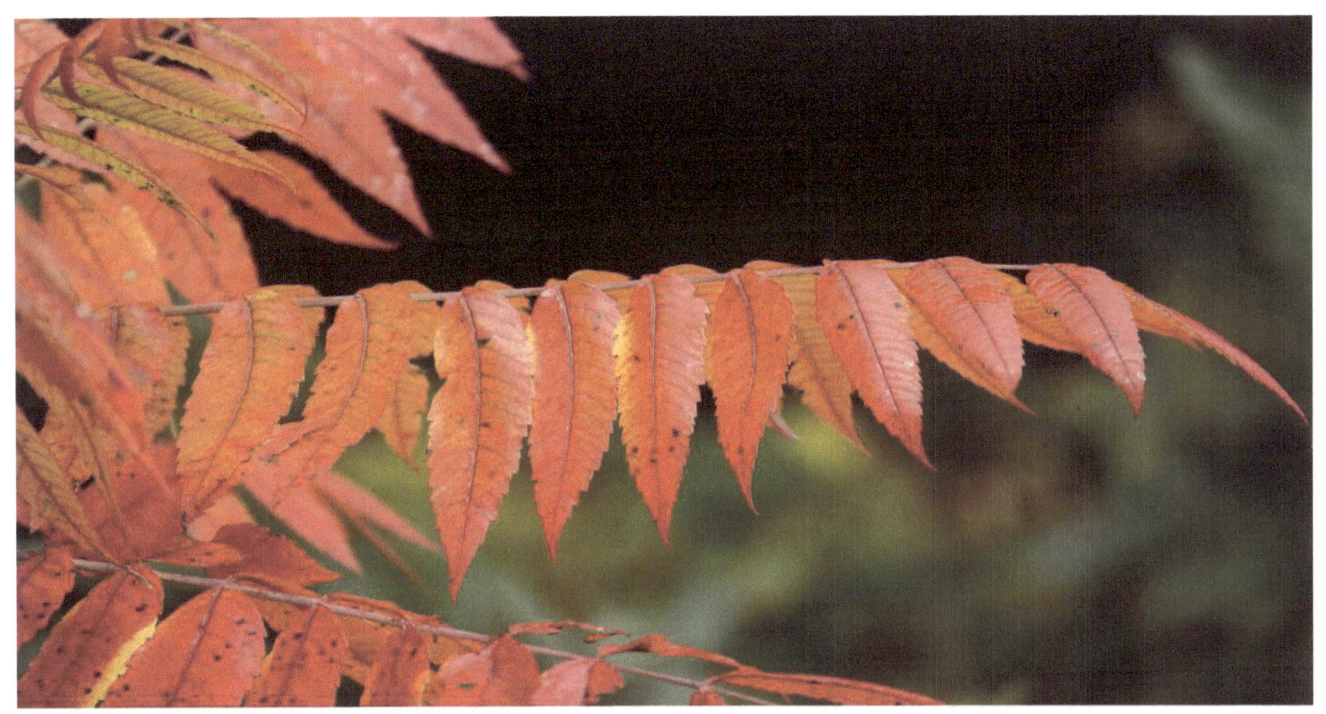

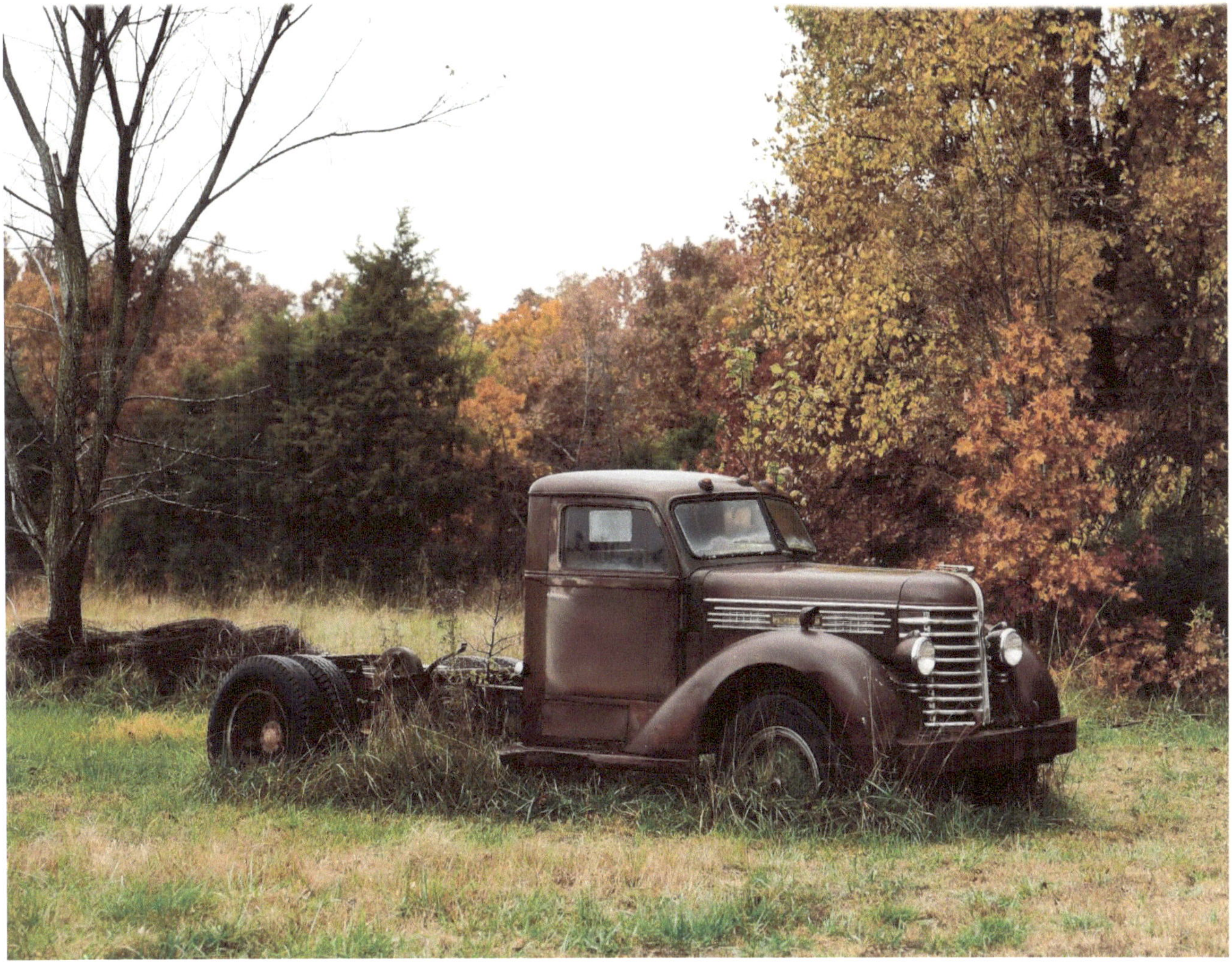

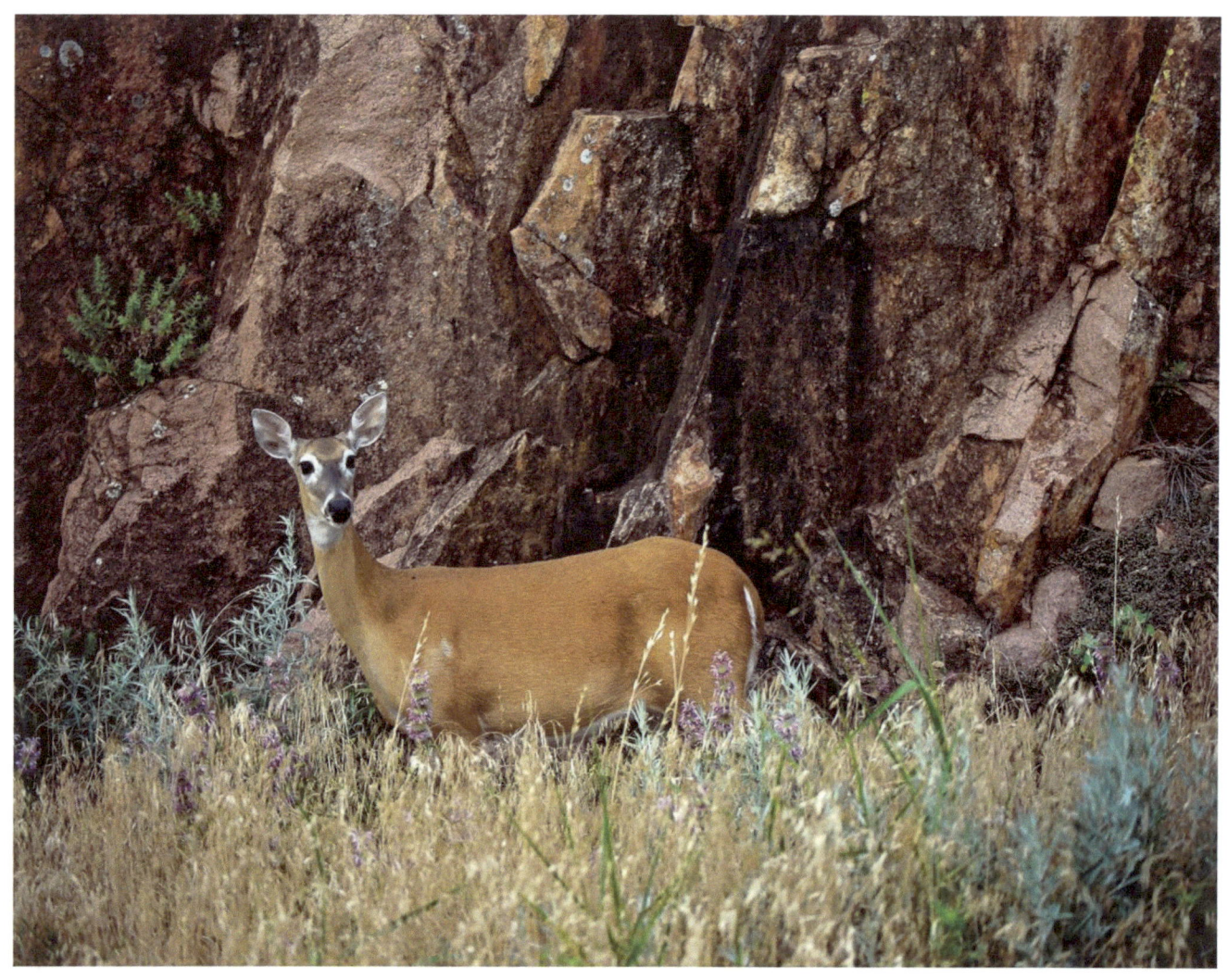

While traveling down a hilly country road,
turned a sharp corner, and
there she was standing close to the road,
as if waiting for me to take her picture.

"Click"   "Got it" !

Nature reveals to us its beauty, glory, power, and creativity.
Thank you God for all that you have created.
We are blessed to be the recipients
of all the beauty that surrounds us.

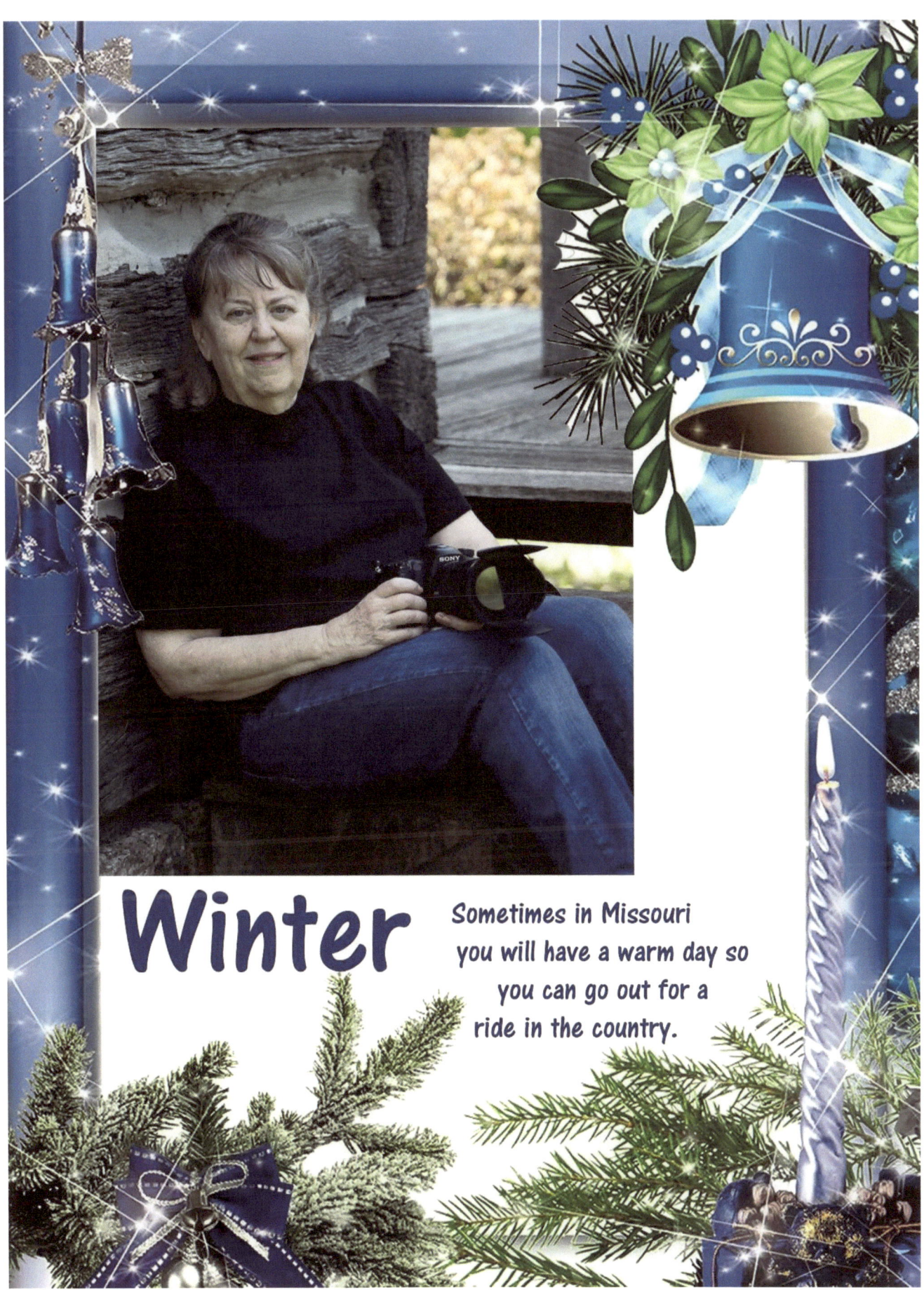

Winter

Sometimes in Missouri you will have a warm day so you can go out for a ride in the country.

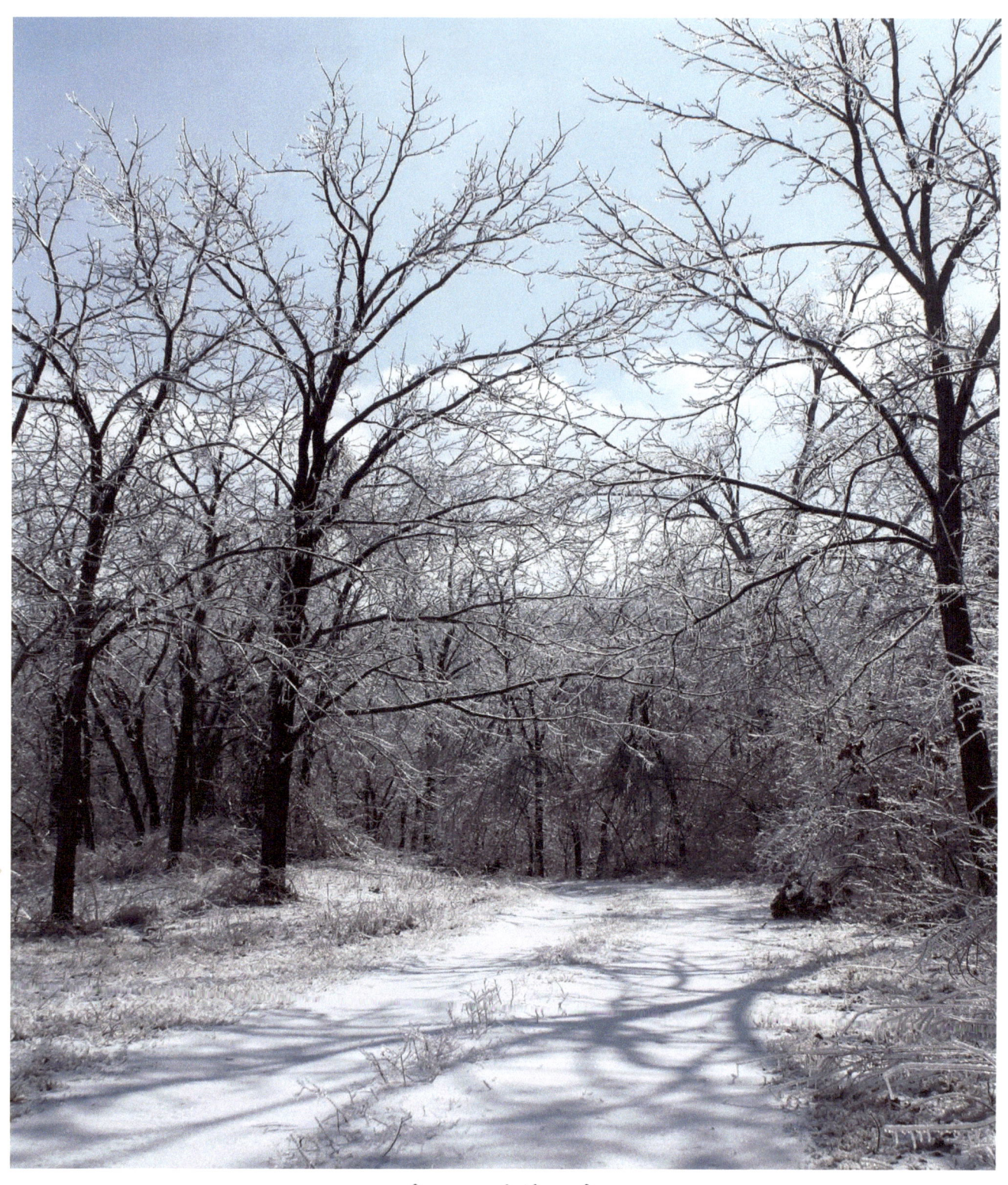

Come on let's go!
We can make it!
Just a little snow and ice.
I'm sure there will be a great photo opportunity just down the hill, around the curve, and over the frozen river.

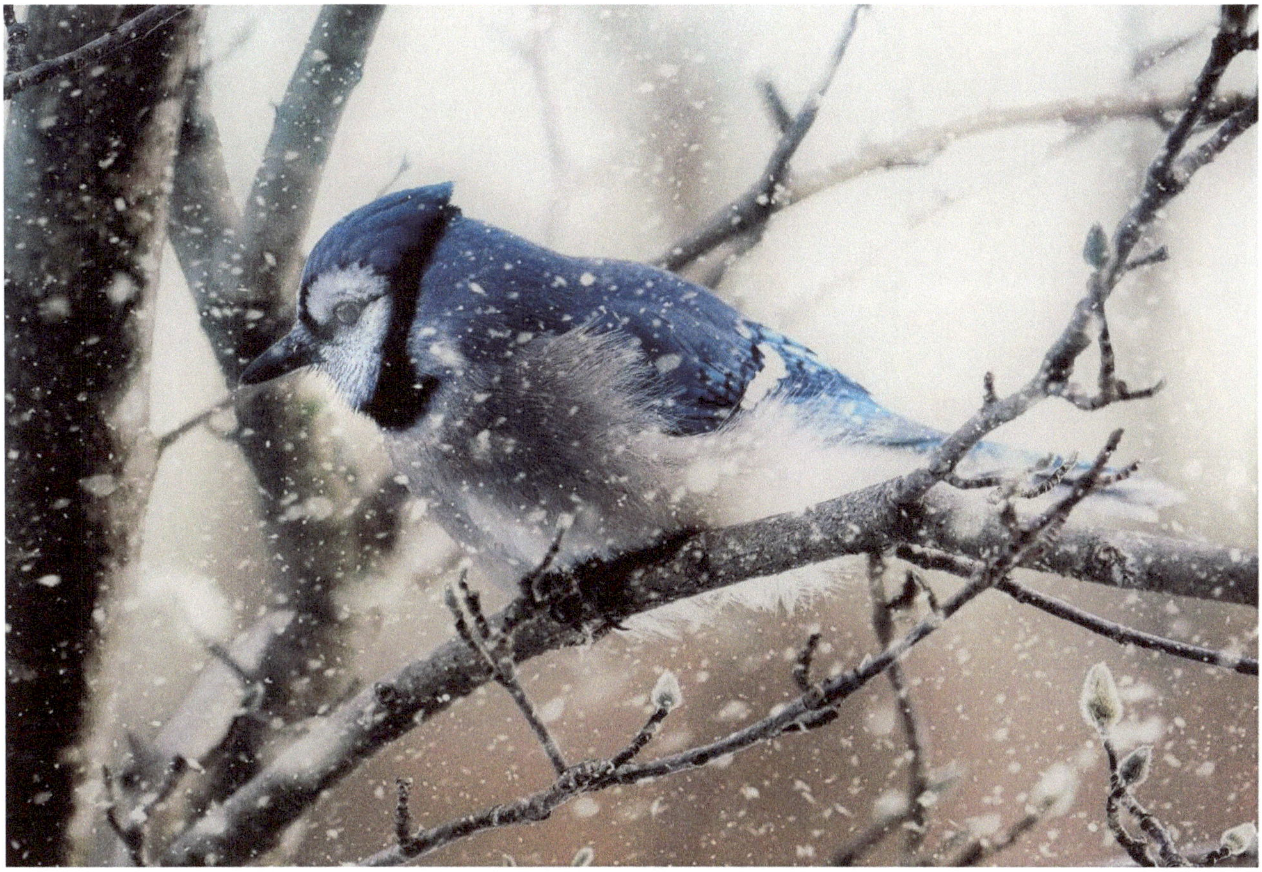

A soft white Winter snow.
Time to go outside and play.

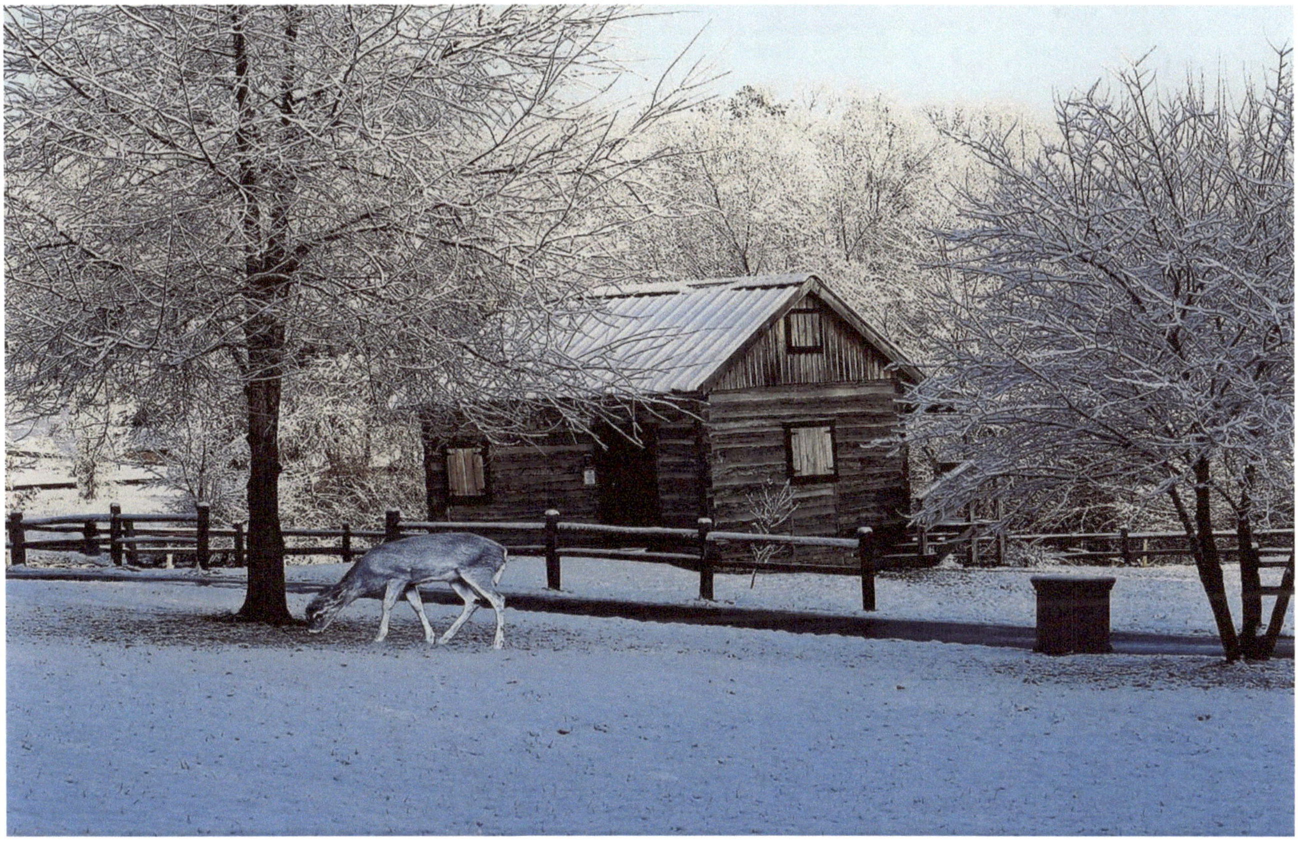

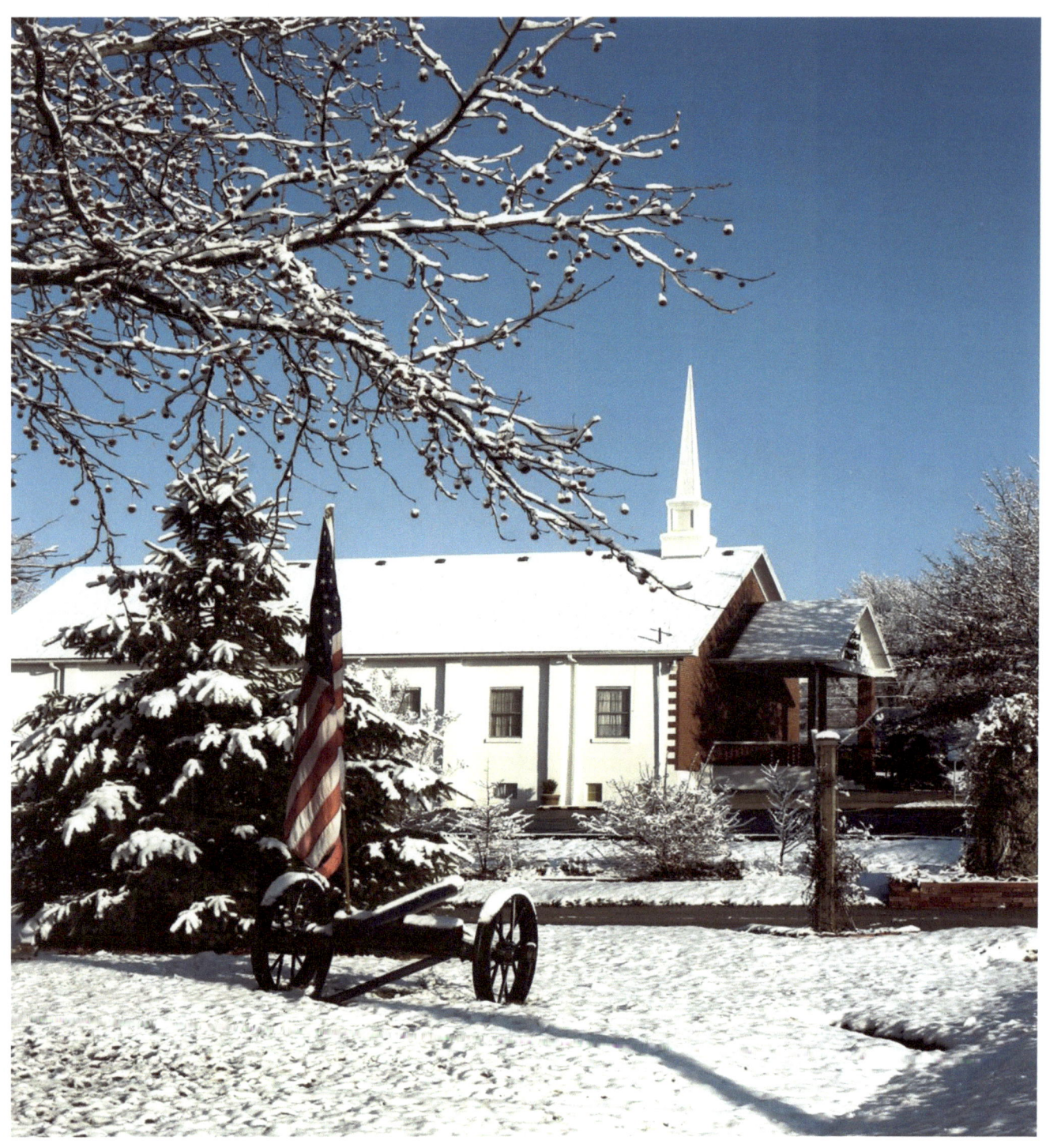

Winter time in the Ozarks can be cold, windy, and snowy.
As a photographer you just have to go out to see
what is covered with white fluffy snow.

I want to share my experiences with people everywhere so
they too can enjoy the wonder of it all.

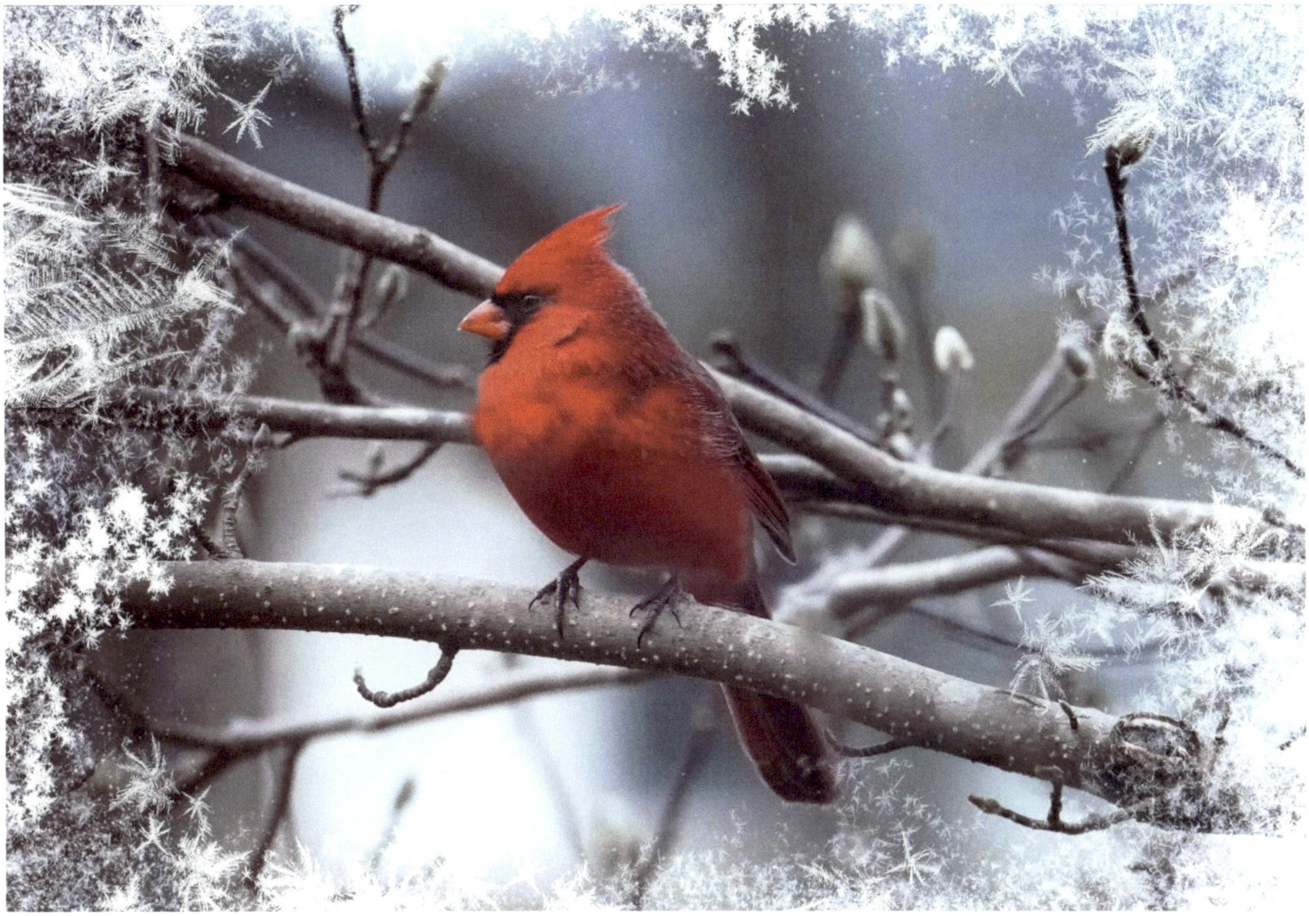

Winter Time in the Ozarks

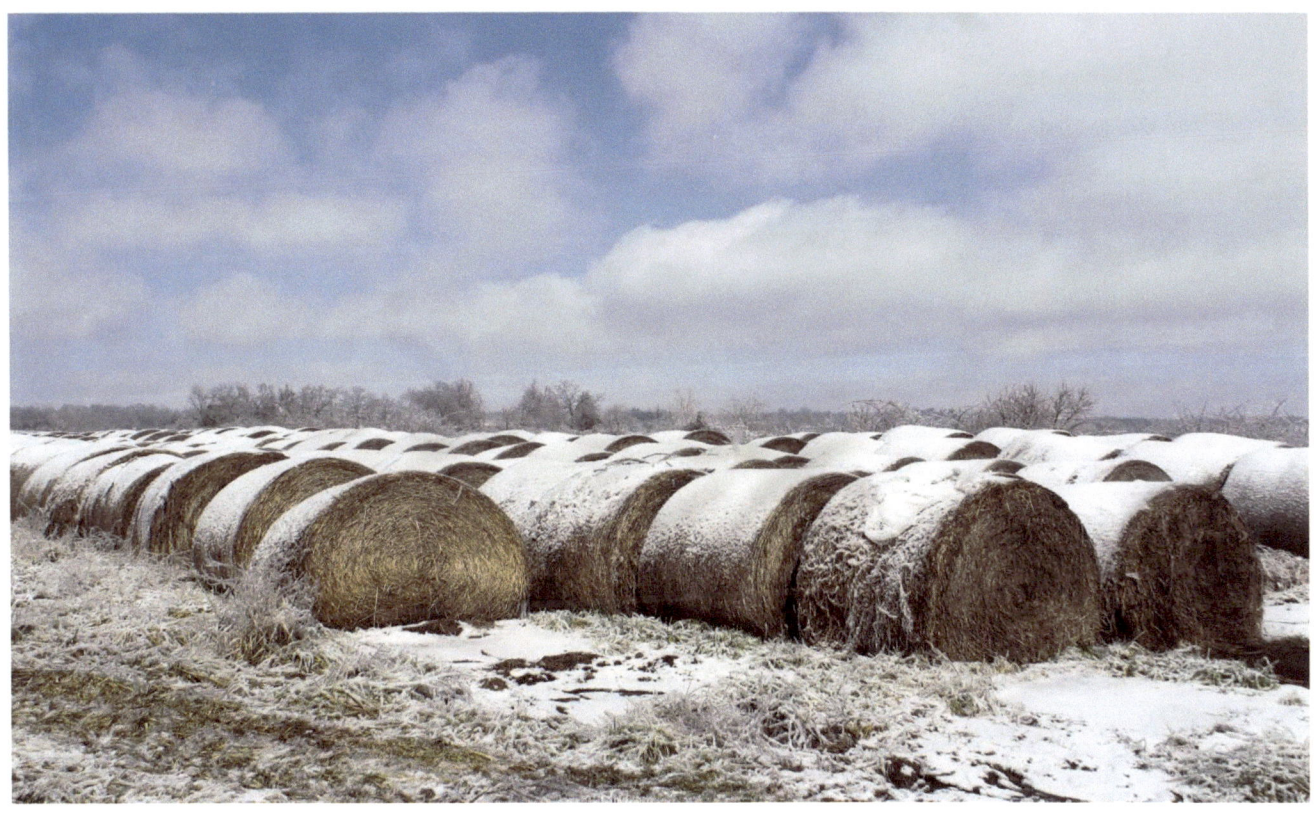

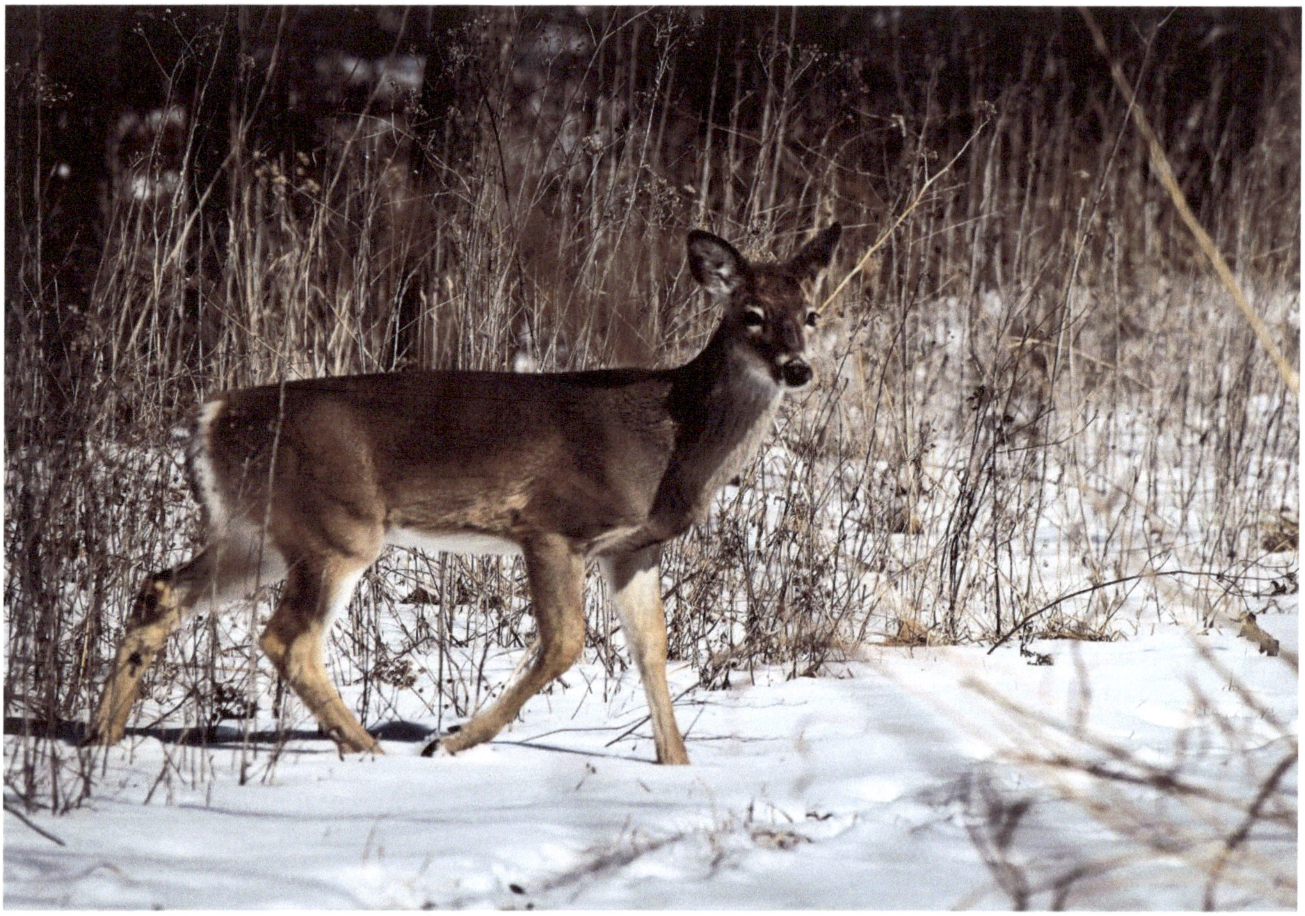

Animals enjoying the sunshine on a cold Winter day.

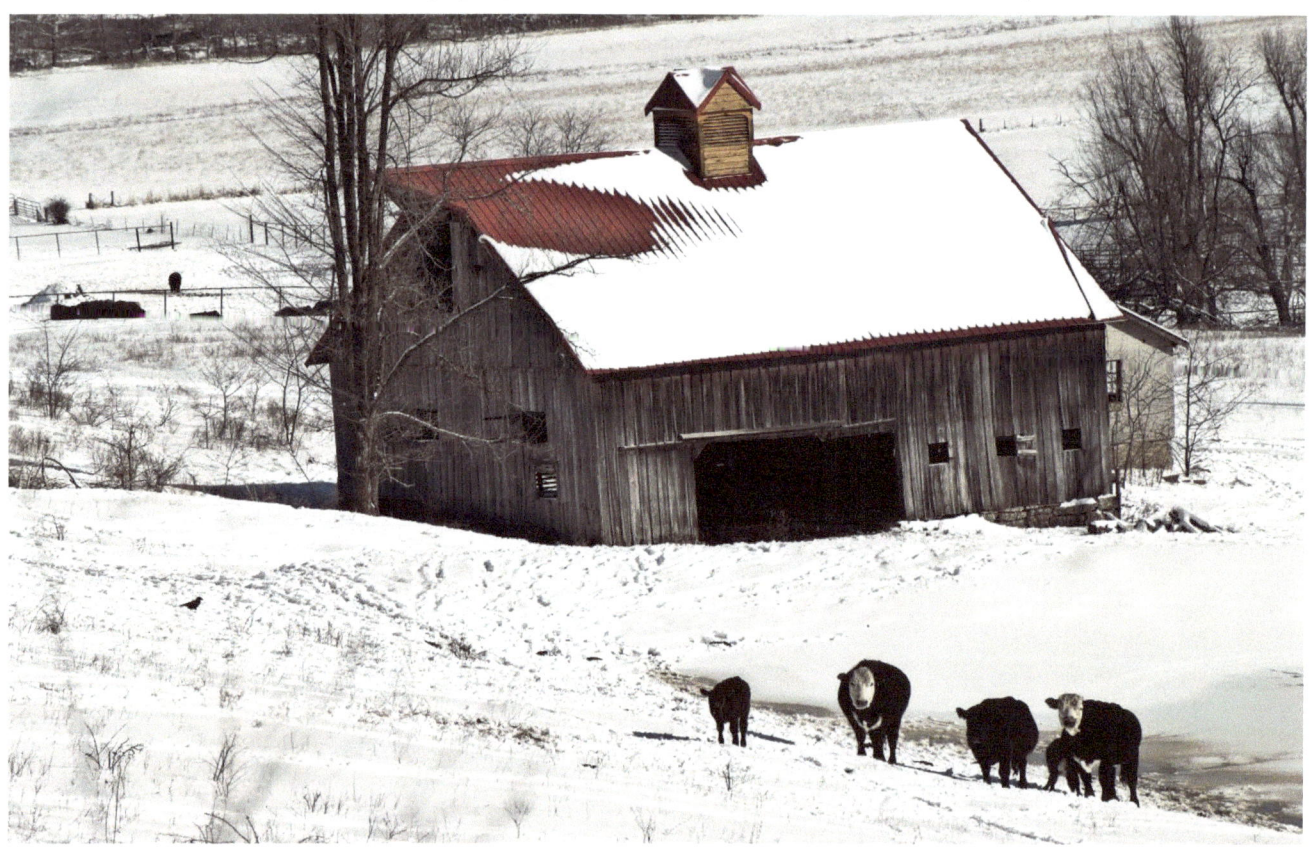

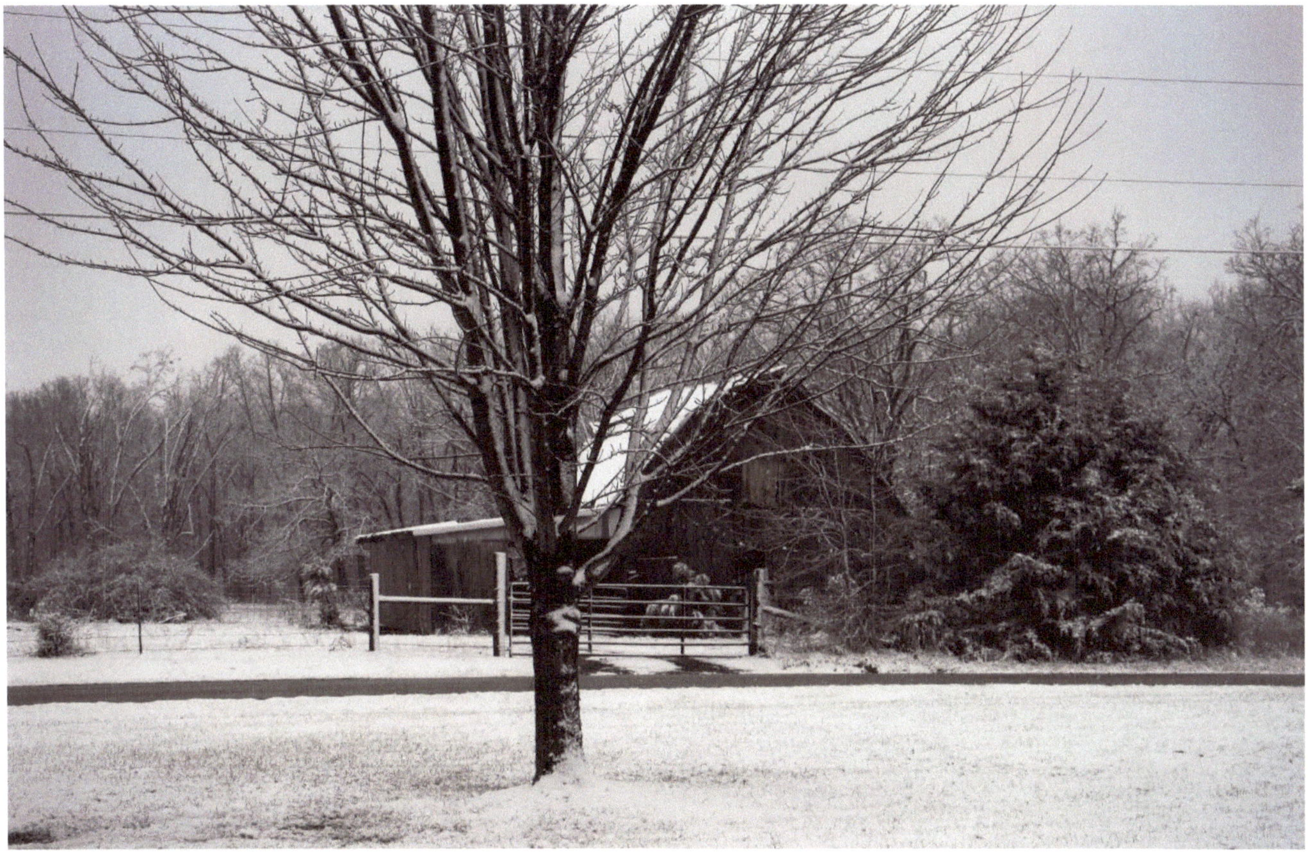

A cold Winter day in the Ozarks

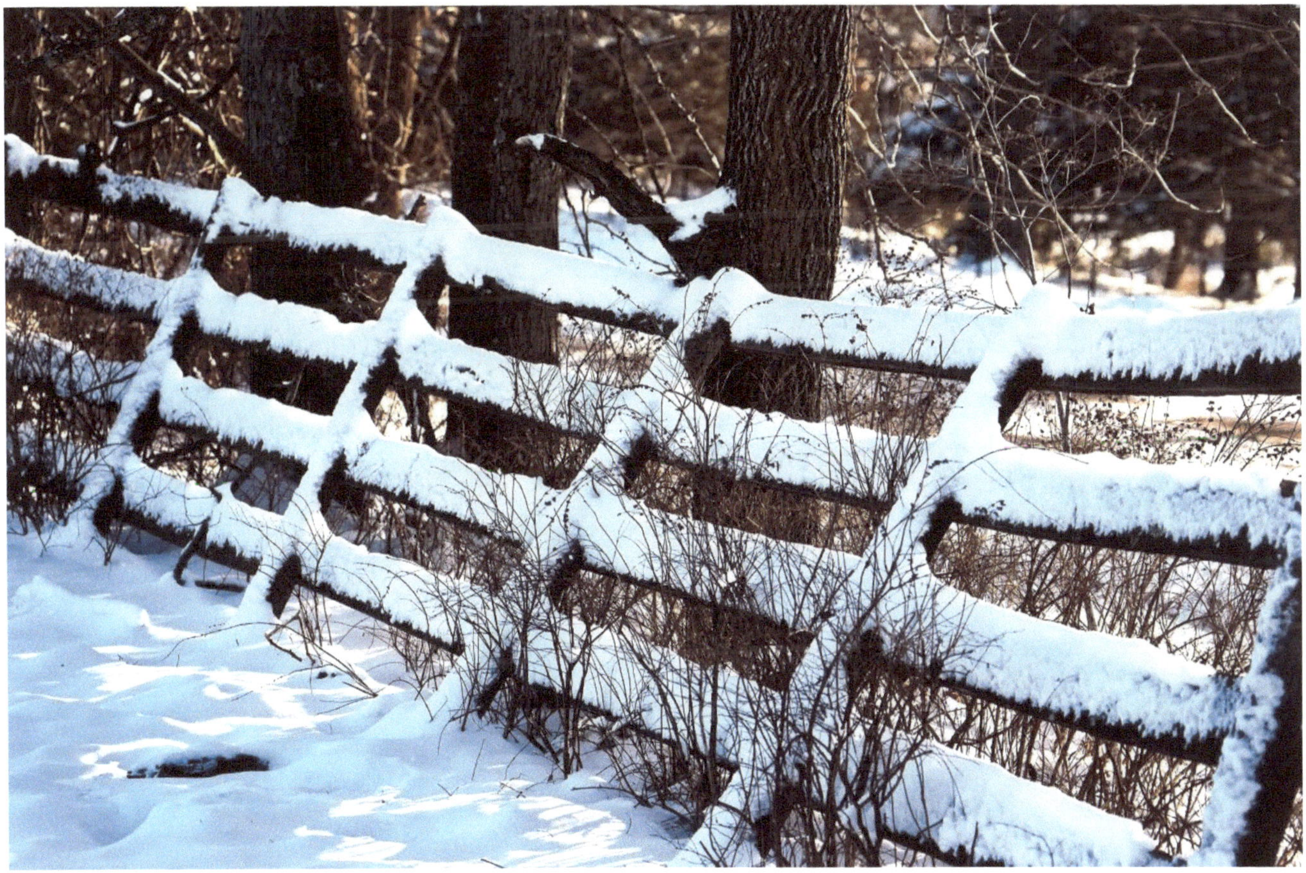

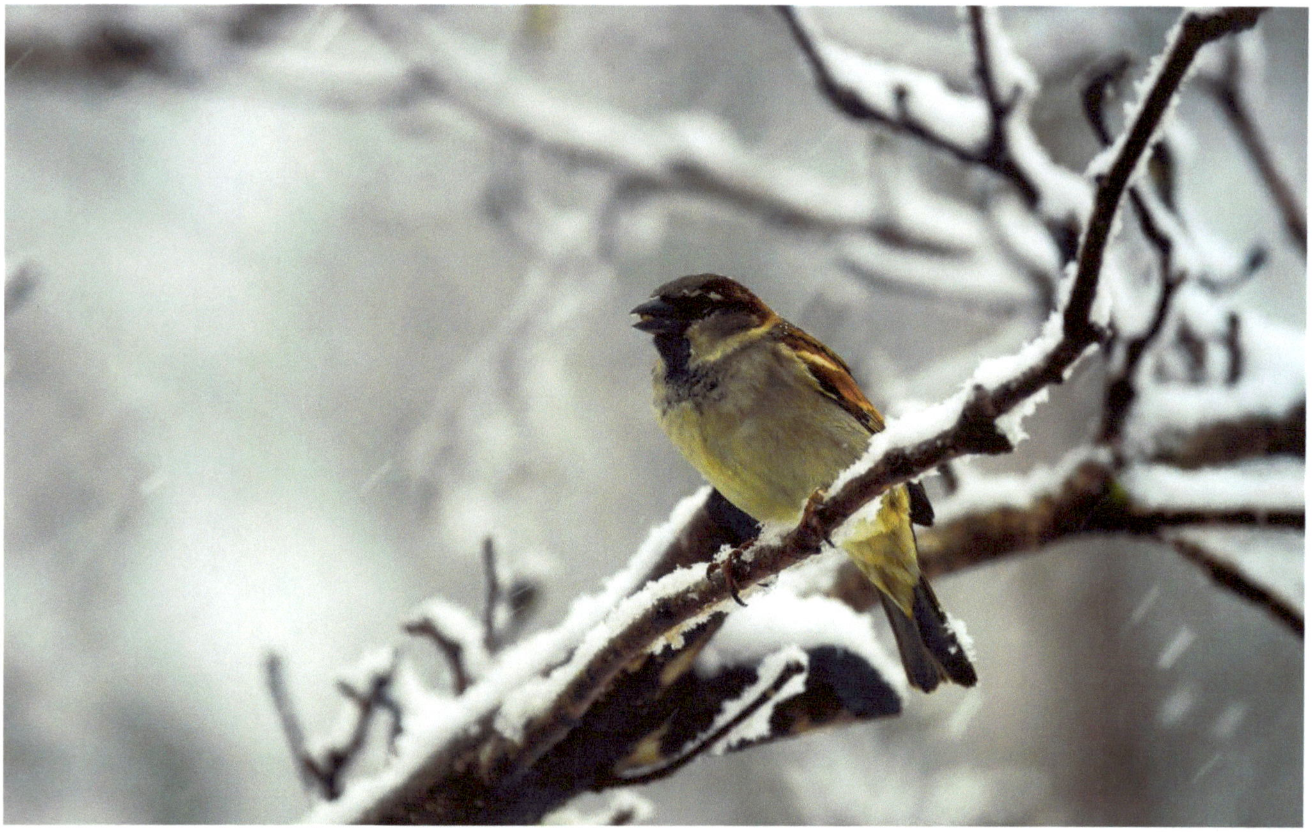

It was a cold, cold day.

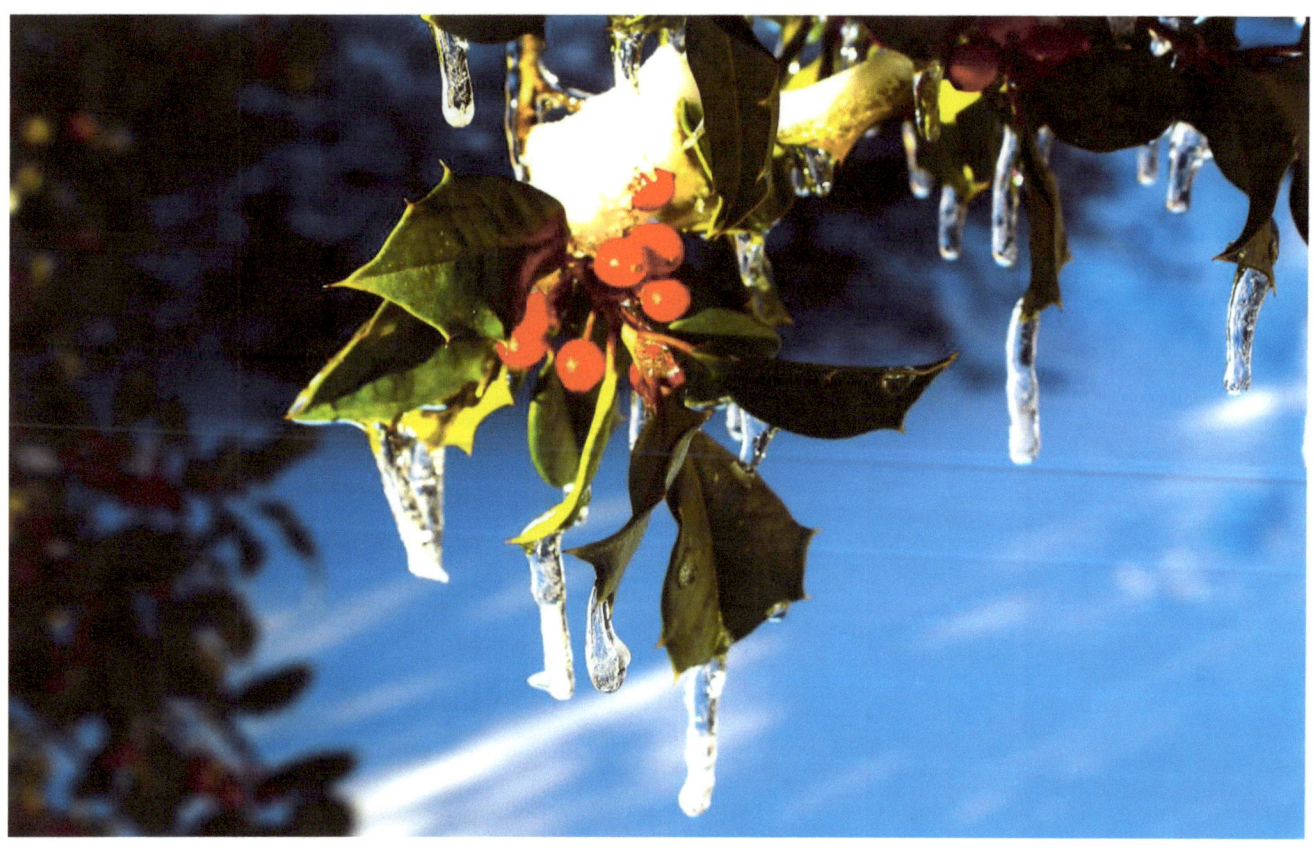

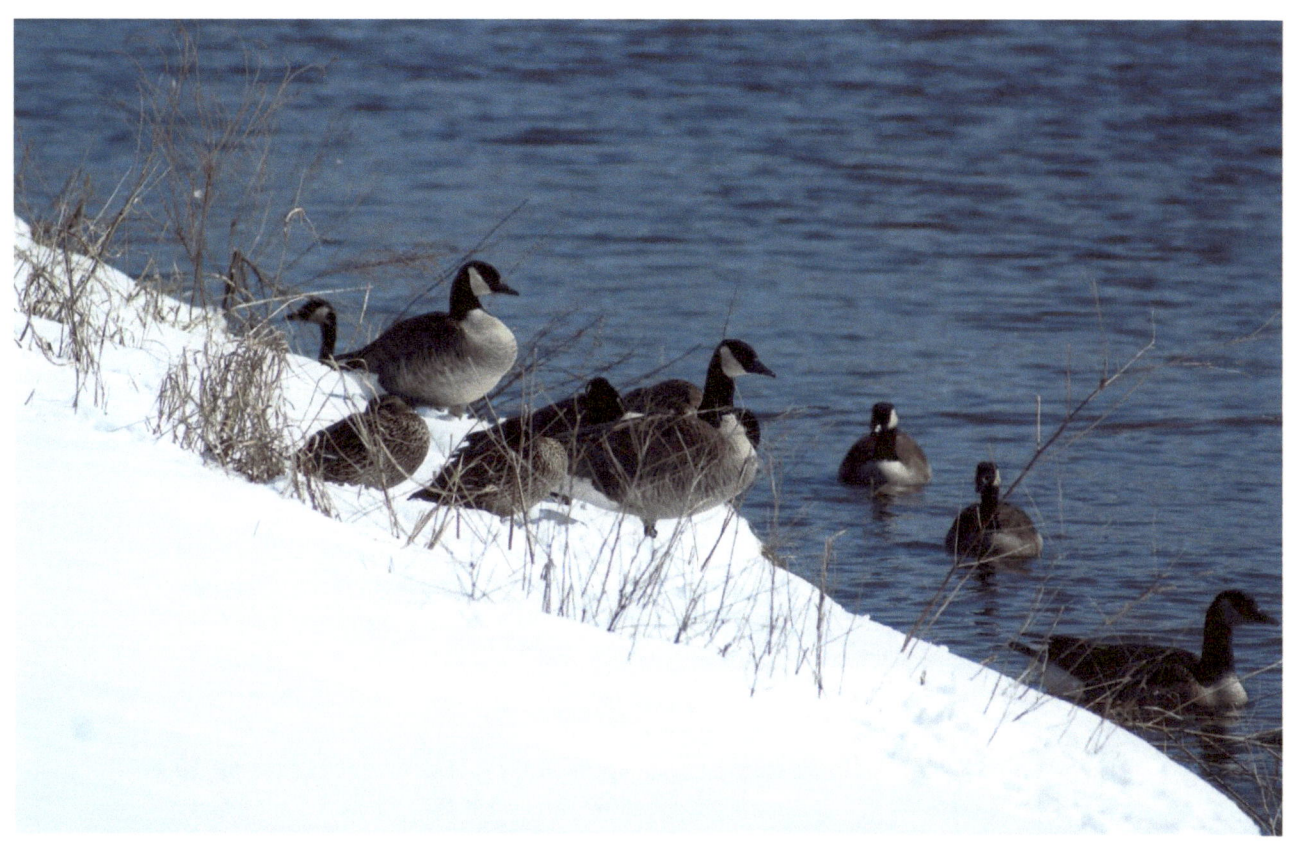

It's a good time to go out and play in the snow.

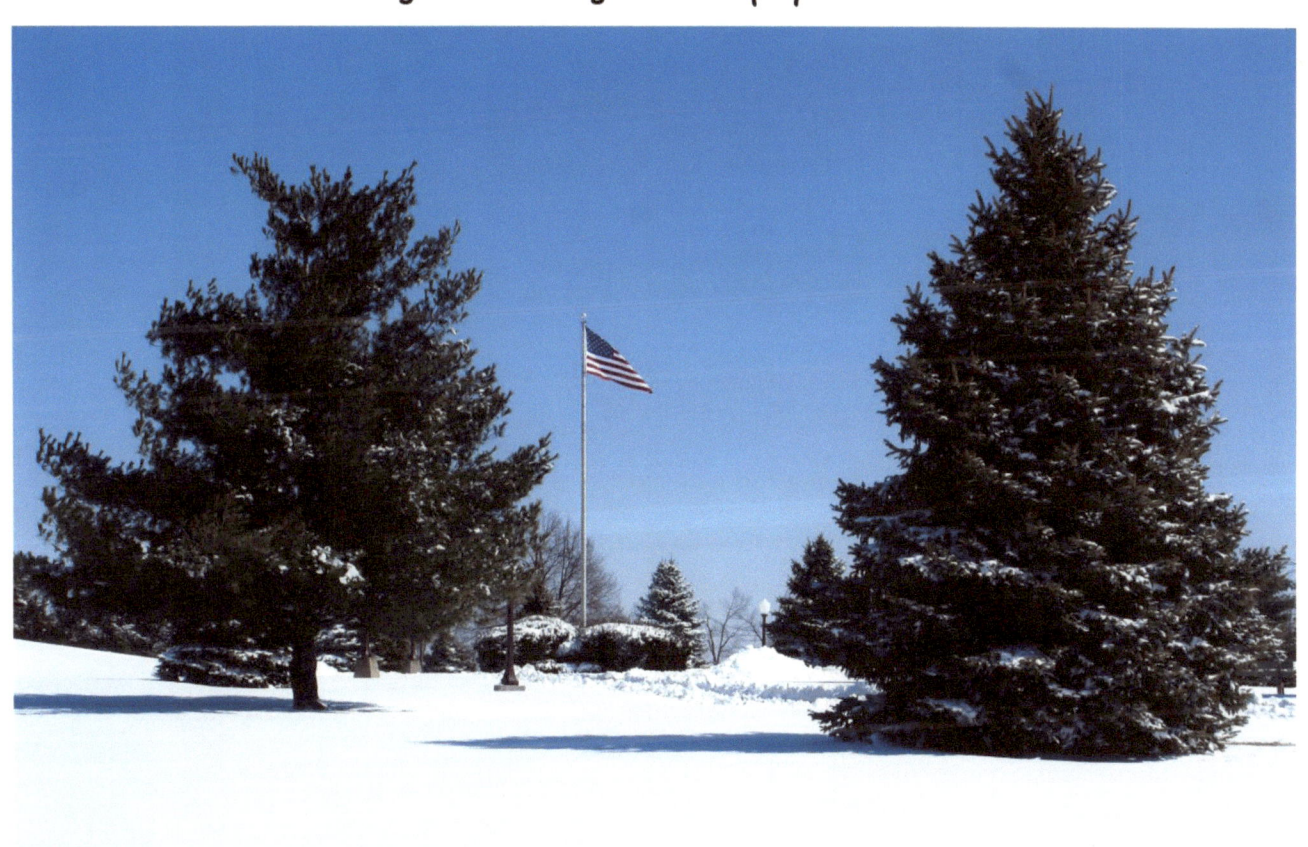

About the Photographer

Rosalie uses her photography passion to capture nature. The creative process starts the moment she looks through the lens of the camera. Her ability to see the beauty and details of nature brings inspiration and joy to her photographs and paintings. She also uses her photo's for ideas for her paintings in oil, acrylic, watercolor, and digital paintings.

She was born and raised in Niangua, Missouri. Married a navy man named Dalton Perryman, also from Niangua, and they traveled throughout the United states as a family with their three children. Life has been action-filled as a wife, mother, retail manger, professional clown, puppeteer, photographer, and artist. She enjoys the performing arts as well as the visual art.

They return to Missouri in 1996 and owned and operated the Jubilee Puppet Theater for 20 years. Rosalie performs her marionette puppet shows throughout the Ozarks and mid-West.

Photographs in this book were taken on roads in the Missouri Ozarks. Edited with Photoshop.

www.ingramcontent.com/pod-product-compliance
Lightning Source LLC
Chambersburg PA
CBHW040409220526
45473CB00004B/1186